Love Unbounded

The Influence of First Baptist Church on Abilene, Texas

Love Unbounded

The Influence of First Baptist Church on Abilene, Texas

By
Rob Fink and Tiffany M. Fink

With Foreword by
Dr. Philip L. Christopher, Senior Pastor
First Baptist Church, Abilene, Texas

State House Press
Buffalo Gap, Texas

Library of Congress Cataloging-in-Publication Data

Fink, Rob (Robert)
Love unbounded : the influence of First Baptist Church on Abilene, Texas / by Rob Fink and Tiffany M. Fink ; with foreword by Philip L. Christopher.
p. cm.
Includes bibliographical references and index.
ISBN 978-1-933337-32-6
1. First Baptist Church (Abilene, Tex.)–History. 2. Abilene (Tex.)–Church history. I. Fink, Tiffany M. II. Title.

BX6480.A25F56 2009
286'.1764727–dc22

2008046315

State House Press
P.O. Box 818
Buffalo Gap, TX 79508
(325) 572-3974
www.mcwhiney.org/press

Distributed by Texas A&M University Press Consortium
(800) 826-8911
www.tamu.edu/upress

Printed in the United States of America

ISBN 978-1-933337-32-6

Book designed by Rosenbohm Graphic Design

Contents

List of Illustrations

All pictures courtesy of First Baptist Church archives unless otherwise noted.

Acknowledgements

Embarking on an adventure of research, writing, and story telling comes to fruition through the efforts of the many, not the few. The resounding chorus echoes through the archives of First Baptist Church, Abilene, Texas. From the first note sung by the chorus of believers in Christ, members laid groundwork, compiled and preserved records, photographs, and various related documents, providing the necessary support requisite for bringing such an endeavor to completion. The experience has left a permanent mark in our memories, just as a sweet melody remains even after the song ends. The 125th Anniversary Committee at First Baptist Abilene deserves much gratitude for the compilation of a very useful chronology and overview of the church's history. Thank you to Dr. Bob Ellis, chair of the committee, as well as the other members: Randall Bingaman, Dr. Phil Christopher, Allan Frizzell, Leland Harden, Carol Manwarren, Sandy McGraw, Bryan Mundy, Charles Richardson, Sondra Seamster, Janlyn Thaxton, Kathy Waters, and Todd Wilson. First Baptist Abilene Librarian, Karin Richardson, allowed continued access to the church archives and provided constant support of the project. Sondra Seamster deserves special mention for her tireless efforts to preserve the archives of First Baptist. Scott and Leah Jeffries, David and Sharon Leyerle, Maewyn Herring, Steve Queen, Scott Cook and Dr. Phil Christopher lent their time and opened their hearts to relay the stories of how God has continued to work through First Baptist Church in the community of Abilene, Texas. Their participation played an integral role in the project. The financial support provided by the First Baptist Foundation to secure digital recorders as well as cover research and publication costs is greatly appreciated. The enthusiasm and other various forms of assistance put forth by Mike Greenfield served to spur us forward and helped to keep the project ever progressing. From the beginning of the project, Mike shared our vision and offered his unwavering support. Dr. Phil Christopher also provided immeasurable support and encouragement as we worked through the documents, sharing our passion about the rich history of First Baptist Abilene. We greatly appreciate Dr. Christopher's work on the foreword of the book. At State House Press, we want to thank Dr. Robert Pace and Dr. Don Frazier. Dr. Pace provided guidance, wisdom and encouragement. Additionally, Dr. Pace designed the map of the mission outreach of First Baptist. Thank you for taking a chance on us on and for supporting our vision. Rob would like to thank McMurry University for their support. Tiffany would like to thank Hardin-Simmons University for encouraging teaching excellence through pursuit of academic endeavors.

Another side effect of projects such as this one is the toll that it takes on a family. At any given time, fifty percent of our household was focused on the book. To Andrew, thank you for reading so skillfully to your younger brother when Mommy and Daddy needed five more minutes to finish a thought. To Dylan, thank you for waiting so patiently for Mommy and Daddy to complete a final sentence before fetching a snack or assisting in the construction of a track for our trains. We greatly value the support of our extended families and friends. Thank you for the innumerable ways in which you helped to bring this story from the archives and into public view. It is His story, the one about love—unbounded, limitless, and beyond all human comprehension.

To God be the glory,
Rob and Tiffany Fink

Foreword

By Dr. Philip Christopher, Senior Pastor

The world and church has obviously changed since 1881 when Abilene was only a tent city and First Baptist Church met for the first time in a school house. In the midst of a changing culture one thing has not changed: First Baptist, Abilene continues the journey of being a people on mission.

Perhaps the terrain of West Texas played a part in nurturing the vision that allowed the church to see new horizons for helping people. The pioneering spirit of those early settlers that ventured to a new frontier was reflected in the pioneer and mission spirit of First Baptist. Yet, the mission story of First Baptist goes beyond the outward landscape or geography to the passion of a people who had a vision for the Kingdom and the world.

Settlers came and built a new community and a new church. However, First Baptist was never content with a settler or status quo mentality. The article in the *Abilene Reporter News* in 1954 highlighted the dedication of the new sanctuary and captured the spirit of the past and a prophecy for our future call to missions: "An evangelistic, progressive, and pioneering church."

The mission story of the church is like a song, captured by the use of hymn titles in each chapter of this book. Some stories can be told with words. This story rises off the pages like the "Doxology" sung with gratitude and awe. The book of Job declares the goodness of God, *"He giveth songs in the night."* The mission story of First Baptist reveals the many ways that this church offered a song of hope and healing to a dark and hurting world.

The faithful song of this story goes on with new arrangements and new singers. But it is still the same song or melody of God's Kingdom. The Family Life Center under the leadership of Scott Cook has expanded its recreational ministry in a mission partnership with Pioneer Drive through *Upward Basketball.* This past year over five hundred children participated in this innovative approach to learning basketball, leadership, and character building in a Christ centered environment. In 2005, the recreation ministry added *Upward Flag Football* which incorporates the same values as basketball. On any Saturday in the fall, more than one thousand players and families gather at Lee Complex and come in contact with the "good news" of Jesus Christ.

In 2004, The Family Life Center converted one of the racquetball courts into a fitness area and expanded the cardiovascular area. This addition provides people with affordable wellness care in comparison to high-priced health clubs. The area resembles a picture of the Kingdom as people from all walks of life, ages, and ethnicities workout side-by- side in friendship and ministry. The emphasis on fitness allows church members to be on mission as they build relationship with people in our community through fitness and reaffirms the original mission of the Family Life Center.

The foresight of the church in planning for a television ministry in the fifties has continued into the new millennium. First Baptist, Abilene was one of the first churches in the United States to broadcast its services on digital High Definition television.

In 2006 the church voted to approve a five-month study concerning our vision for missions. The recommendation the church approved brought City Light under the budget of the church and called for new bridges of involvement to be built between City Light and the church. It called for the creation of a new position, Pastor for Missions, that would coordinate the work of City Light and provide global missional opportunities for the entire congregation.

A new vision of missions began to grow out of this study and vote. Under the leadership of our Pastor for Missions, John Moore, the church is being challenged to look to the next "frontier" of becoming a missional congregation as opposed to a mission-minded church. The missional church centers everything it does around its participation in God's mission in the world as it calls each member to missions and being the presence of Christ. The vision for the future that challenges each member to live out a missional lifestyle has its roots in the soil and soul of a people that planted an outpost for the Kingdom back in December 1881.

As Senior Pastor of this remarkable church, I want to express my deep appreciation to Doctors Rob and Tiffany Fink for taking on the task of writing a history of missions for First Baptist, Abilene. The book reveals much more than dates and significant events. It goes beyond offering a chronology of the church's history. The book captures the character and community of a frontier people committed to sharing the love of Christ. The authors are artists that weave together the colored threads of the stories and people into a stunning tapestry of missions which provides a vibrant picture of our past.

Things have changed. The sound of the westward whistle of the T&P passenger train no longer blows as it pulls in to the old depot. The sound of today is the fast moving traffic whizzing by on Interstate 20 or the blast from B-1's taking off at Dyess.

But some things never change. The song of this church that has echoed over the prairie for one hundred and twenty-seven years can still be heard. How overwhelming to think of the number of people over the years that have sung this song and the thousands of lives that have been changed because they heard this song of God's love. The song still goes on as we sing in gratitude for the past and hope for the future, *"God of grace and God of glory, On Thy people pour Thy pow'r; Crown Thy ancient church's story, Bring her bud to glorious flower."*

Brave Journey,
Philip L. Christopher, D.Min.
Senior Pastor

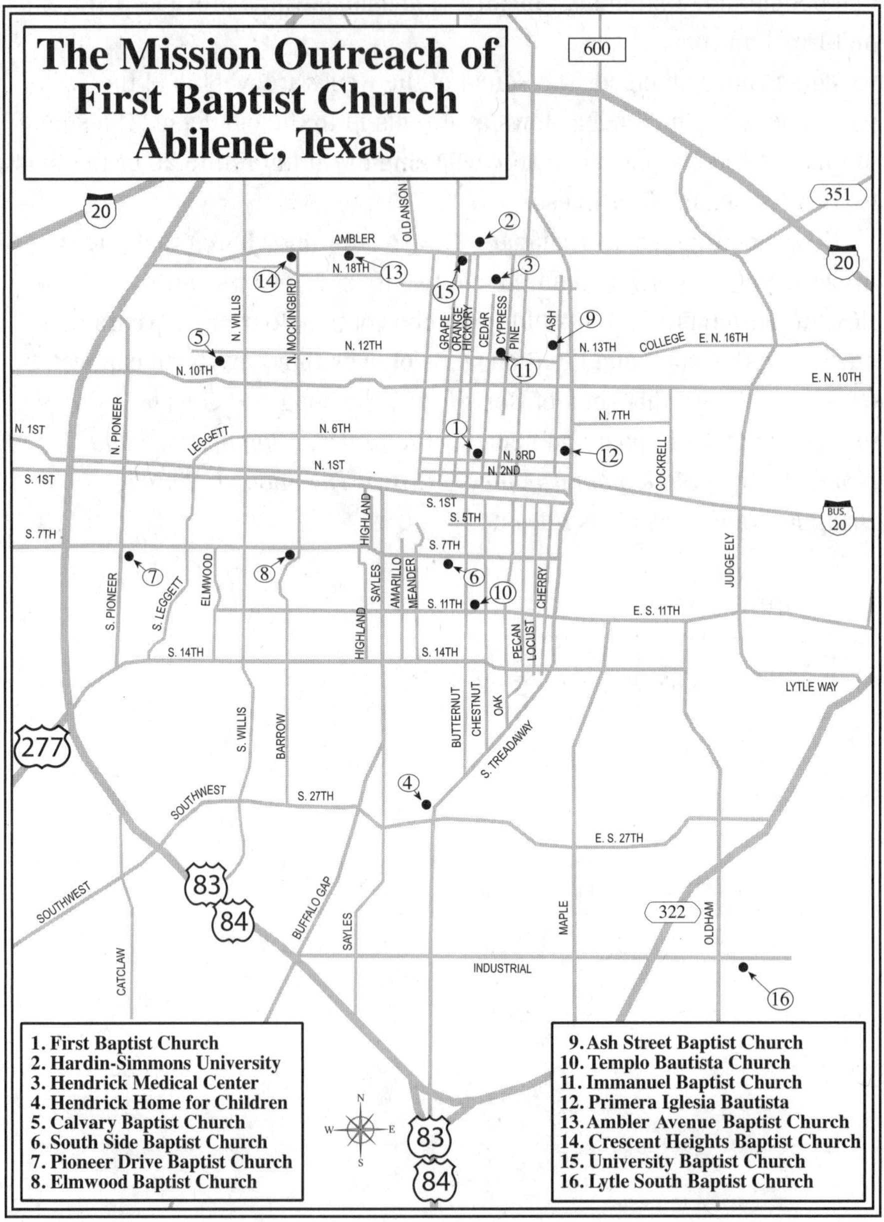
The Mission Outreach of
First Baptist Church
Abilene, Texas
600
351
20
AMBLER
OLD ANSON
N. 18TH
N. WILLIS
N. MOCKINGBIRD
GRAPE
ORANGE
HICKORY
CEDAR
CYPRESS
PINE
ASH
N. 12TH
N. 10TH
N. 13TH
COLLEGE
E. N. 16TH
E. N. 10TH
N. 7TH
N. 1ST
N. PIONEER
LEGGETT
N. 6TH
N. 3RD
N. 2ND
COCKRELL
S. 1ST
S. 5TH
BUS. 20
S. 7TH
HIGHLAND
SAYLES
AMARILLO
MEANDER
S. PIONEER
S. LEGGETT
ELMWOOD
S. 11TH
CHERRY
E. S. 11TH
JUDGE ELY
S. 14TH
PECAN
LOCUST
LYTLE WAY
BUTTERNUT
CHESTNUT
OAK
S. WILLIS
BARROW
S. TREADAWAY
277
SOUTHWEST
S. 27TH
E. S. 27TH
83
84
BUFFALO GAP
MAPLE
322
OLDHAM
CATCLAW
INDUSTRIAL
N
W
E
S
1. First Baptist Church
2. Hardin-Simmons University
3. Hendrick Medical Center
4. Hendrick Home for Children
5. Calvary Baptist Church
6. South Side Baptist Church
7. Pioneer Drive Baptist Church
8. Elmwood Baptist Church
9. Ash Street Baptist Church
10. Templo Bautista Church
11. Immanuel Baptist Church
12. Primera Iglesia Bautista
13. Ambler Avenue Baptist Church
14. Crescent Heights Baptist Church
15. University Baptist Church
16. Lytle South Baptist Church

Introduction

The founders of Abilene envisioned a city of greatness, prompting those visionaries to name their West Texas home after the great Kansas cattle town of the late nineteenth century. Cattle, however, did not make this Texas community great. People did.

Many personalities played key roles in establishing institutions in what was once a frontier settlement on the western edge of a dangerous and rugged part of Texas. But few were more important than the enthusiastic, hard-working individuals associated with what became the First Baptist Church of Abilene. For well over a century, members of one of the city's oldest congregations worked to meet the needs of area residents. The connection between Abilene and First Baptist Church became a strong one. The congregation served as a nexus of community growth, services, development, and outreach in the city's early days.

The founders of First Baptist Church set out to meet the various needs of the fledgling community. That missionary spirit remained a guiding principle as the institution grew and became more intimately connected with the people of Abilene.

Over the years, First Baptist established organizations and programs to help the town. Groups such as the Willing Workers and the Women's Mission Union organized fundraisers and clothing drives and collected food for the needy in Abilene—members and nonmembers.

The overall focus of First Baptist's ministry remained on the people of Abilene. Even though the church participated in outreach opportunities during two world wars and the Great Depression, the congregation continually offered assistance through programs designed to meet physical and spiritual needs, whether the demands of history required it or not. First Baptist was founded with a mission-oriented focus that emphasized local missions in particular, which played a vital role in the establishment of the city.

This focus on local missions resulted in several important projects initiated by the church membership. First Baptist worked to establish the town's first institution of higher education, an effort that ultimately produced Hardin-Simmons University. A few decades later, the need for quality health care drew the church's attention and led to the creation of the West Texas Baptist Sanitarium, which later became Hendrick Memorial Hospital. The final significant local institution born out of the work of First Baptist, Abilene was the Hendrick Home for Children, created to provide housing and non-medical care for children throughout West Texas.

The influence of First Baptist on Abilene's growth extended beyond these major institutions. The church also continually founded missions throughout the town as Abilene's population grew. The missions eventually became independent churches, resulting in the addition of more than eighteen Baptist congregations in the area.

As Abilene's population increased in the post-World War II era, First Baptist looked to redefine its role as a downtown church. As a result, it created new mission outreach programs to help its own members as well as others within the community. As Abilenians entered the 1970s, women made up a significant portion of the nations' workforce, increasing the need for affordable, quality child care. Additionally, the institution of marriage became strained nationwide, revealing an opportunity for ministry to struggling couples and families through Christian counseling. Recreation ministry evolved as a way to bring families together through sports and games in a Christ-centered environment. And the homeless population in Abilene grew at an exponential rate, exposing the need for more aggressive outreach to the city's less fortunate.

Certainly, the modern city of Abilene, Texas, held as many missionary opportunities as the dusty, fledgling town of the late nineteenth century. First Baptist Abilene met the challenges with a pioneering spirit, a missionary focus, and a deeply held conviction: "On Christ the Solid Rock I stand / All other ground is sinking sand / All other ground is sinking sand."

Chapter I

"They Will Know We Are Christians By Our Love"

The growth of Abilene was arguably more a matter of people than place. The region offered no natural resources or economic enticements for growth, such as large supplies of water or oil reserves. As a result, Abilene grew because of its residents' efforts. And given the centrality of this human element, First Baptist Church played a significant role in the town's history. Its mission efforts focused on assisting the church itself, meeting the community's physical needs, and addressing the town's spiritual concerns. The daily work of First Baptist directly influenced the growth of Abilene.

As in so much of West Texas, the area's population predated the city per se. The region's original inhabitants were nomads. Native American peoples, specifically the Comanche and Kiowa, migrated throughout the area, hunting buffalo and other food sources. The Butterfield Overland Stage line traversed the region as it carried goods between California and the eastern United States. Cowmen who tended small herds of cattle, usually on foot, passed through West Texas, as did the large cattle drives along the Great Western Trail on their way to railroad lines and markets in Kansas.[1]

Many of the Abilene area's early settlers first came to the region in the 1870s to hunt buffalo. Several of these hunters, including John B. Clack, later returned to the area with their families to live. Clack's niece Tommie Lou

Clack recalled a story that her uncle told concerning how he and another hunter, A.J. Turner, became trapped in Elm Creek amid a stampede of buffalo in an area that later fell within the Abilene city limits.[2] These men later returned to the area to establish homesteads and small ranches. Ranchers gradually populated the region, and when the Texas and Pacific Railroad Company (T&P) proposed the construction of a line through the area, the potential for a developed community appealed to early settlers. But builders with the T&P encountered a series of challenges before reaching Abilene.

After receiving a congressional charter in 1871, the builders announced plans to construct a line connecting Marshall in East Texas with San Diego, California. Grenville M. Dodge, formerly employed by the Union Pacific Railroad, served as chief engineer. Dodge in turn contracted the construction work to Morgan Jones, who built west from Marshall until the economic crisis of 1873 forced the company to halt construction in the Fort Worth area.[3]

The T&P's proposed line to California lay dormant for the next seven years, except for a change in ownership. A group of East Coast financiers led by Jay Gould bought the railroad. Gould, long connected with railroad construction and operation in the United States, revived the T&P's westward march. Motivated by the potential competition for U.S. land grants with rival C.P. Huntington and his Southern Pacific Railroad, Gould pushed the westbound project forward. T&P track construction, therefore, progressed at a dramatic pace.[4]

Desiring maximum profits, T&P executives proposed the establishment of towns along the new route. The sale of town sites and home lots offered the company the possibility of added wealth. Specifically, Gould and the T&P executives wanted to build a "Future Great City of West Texas."[5] West Texas lacked a major railhead to serve as a prime shipping point for cattle to slaughterhouses in Chicago. Additionally, the undeveloped region needed a distribution center for manufactured goods to surrounding towns and inhabitants as the area became more populated.[6]

The specifics of establishing the town went to J. Stoddard Johnston, a nephew of Civil War Gen. Albert Sidney Johnston. As the representative of the T&P, Johnston met with a group of local ranchers led by John Merchant. Under the terms of the final agreement, the landowners sold the railroad company land on which to build a depot, sidings, and cattle pens at seventy-five cents an acre—half of the base price for the surrounding land. In return, the T&P created town blocks, lots, streets, and alleys. Both parties agreed to divide equally the profits derived from public land sales. Representatives entered into a contract on December 18, 1880, and named the new town "Abilene" after the famous Kansas cattle town, in hopes of becoming equally successful.[7]

On March 15, 1881, Stoddard oversaw the first public auction of town lots, thereby establishing the city's official birth date. People began moving to Abilene before the auction, though. Several hundred lived in tents around the railroad tracks, waiting to purchase home sites. The city's first doctor, W.M. Berry, set up shop in one of the many tents in February 1881, as did the first organized denominational church, First Presbyterian.[8]

The first train to reach Abilene on the new T&P tracks arrived on February 27, 1881. Mary Hampton Clack, one of the town's earliest settlers, recorded one of the only known accounts of the locomotive's arrival: "When the first passenger train rolled into the little canvas town of Abilene, it created almost as much excitement among the inhabitants of the place and country round about, as alarm among the cattle and horses grazing near the track."

Clack added, "The people who had been craning their necks, and straining their eyes for a glimpse of the iron horse, yelled themselves hoarse when the first faint glimmer of light shot over a rise on the mesquite prairie east of town. This was enough to cause a stampede among the dumb brutes."[9]

Once the auction ended, residents engaged in an informal discussion and elected to create the first public school. As the meeting closed, a hat circulated the room for building donations. Nine months later, in that school house, local Baptists met to organize the first Baptist congregation in Abilene.

The man most responsible for the creation of First Baptist Church was Owen C. Pope. A missionary from Lampasas, Pope traveled throughout West Texas establishing churches. He officially worked as the corresponding secretary and superintendent of state missions for the Texas Baptist General Convention as well as the field secretary for the Baptist Church Edifice Department of the American Home Mission Board of New York City.[11]

Pope later wrote of his first experience in Abilene. In 1882 in the *Texas Baptist Herald*, a statewide Baptist newspaper, Pope stated, "We left Runnels with a brisk norther blowing, and rode along admiring the beautiful country

Rev. Owen C. Pope, Founder of First Baptist

lying between Runnels and Abilene . . . At Cedar Gap we spent the night, and by dinner the next day we arrived at the new town of Abilene." He added: "A few months ago the place where Abilene now is, was simply a broad prairie. The T and P Railroad passed through, and a town sprang up as by magic, now containing about 1500 inhabitants, and growing every day . . . I have great hopes that a good Baptist church will soon build up at Abilene."[12]

In founding First Baptist, Pope received aid from many people in Abilene. A key player was C.E. Gilbert, the editor of the recently established *Abilene Reporter News*. Gilbert's wife was a Baptist, and at her urging as well as that of Pope, Gilbert sent word to area Baptists about starting a church. Reverend T.R. Legett, the Baptist preacher in the nearby community of Buffalo Gap, attended the organizational meeting in the school building.[13]

On December 17, 1881, the seventeen original members signed the charter for the new church. The following week, the new congregation held its first service, again at the town's school. M.H. Jones, a traveling missionary, served as the first preacher, receiving a salary of $100 a year. John R. Spaulding, a machinist and early auto dealer in town, served as a deacon and the first Sunday school superintendent.[14]

The young town grew quickly, as did the church. Pope, because of his job as a missionary, left Abilene shortly after the establishment of First Baptist and continued to travel throughout West Texas. In February 1882, he returned to Abilene from El Paso. Upon seeing the congregation still meeting in the schoolhouse, Pope urged members to build a permanent building of their own. As a result, church leaders appointed a board of trustees to select a location.[15]

In 1883, the congregation purchased two lots at North Third and Cedar streets from the T&P Railroad. It look a full year to secure the land, but the church finally received the deed to the lot on July 24, 1883, for $50, and the church built its first building. When the construction was finished in November of that year, Pope described the building as the "best Baptist house of worship on the Texas & Pacific west of Fort Worth."[16]

W.M. Gough, a preacher who wrote about Abilene for the *Texas Baptist Herald,* echoed Pope's sentiment when he described a First Baptist service in 1883: "On Sunday morning we had, it is said, the largest congregation ever assembled in Abilene. It was as fine looking an assembly as the State of Texas affords and they gave good attention to the preaching as could be wished . . . the Baptists of Abilene are now on a permanent footing and will move up their building enterprise."[17]

The original First Baptist Church building, 1883

One early question revolved around equipment for the new church—specifically, the process and resources for acquiring a church bell, an organ, and hymnbooks for the new building. Ultimately, the congregation voted to empower the women of the church to carry out all financial matters related to physical needs.[18]

The work of church members shaped the history of Abilene, but the original First Baptist Church building also played an important role. The sanctuary provided one of the largest indoor meeting places in the area, as well as the first indoor baptistery in town. The church voted to build the baptistery at the urging of a couple of deacons' wives who were immersed in nearby Cedar Creek on a cold winter's day.[19]

With its building in place, the congregation sought to establish its identity within the Baptist faith. Encouraged by the missionary heritage of the

Willing Workers class reunion, 1949

church's founder, members decided on an identity that involved an evangelical focus and a mission mind-set. The church followed the Great Commission in Matthew 28:18–20, where Jesus urged his followers to "go and make disciples of all nations, baptizing them in the name of the Father and the Son and of the Holy Spirit."[20] As a result, annual revivals were conducted, expanding the membership. The organization of the Sunday school in December 1883 further extended the church's evangelistic reach.[21]

Early Sunday school classes focused on the mission aspect of Baptist doctrine and worked to minister to the new town. One class, the Willing Workers, accepted a charge from the congregation's leadership that the "sisters" raise money for the church. As a result, the class took an active role in First Baptist and the Abilene community. Organized in 1894 as a class for single young women between sixteen and twenty years old, the Willing Workers raised funds through ice cream socials, pie socials, chili suppers, and tamale suppers.[22]

For the ice cream socials, the young women in the group borrowed a horse and buggy and drove around the community collecting donations of milk, eggs, and sugar. They then sold the finished product for fifteen cents per bowl. Led by Mrs. M.H. Compere, the Willing Workers used the proceeds for a wide array of purposes. They funded a balcony and a stained-glass window in the sanctuary, and a few years later, in 1898, they raised $65 to help purchase new carpet for the church building.[23]

The annual church revival also served as a primary method of outreach. At the end of November and the beginning of December 1884, First Baptist held a two-week revival. Frank Kiefer, one of the most famous evangelists of the 1880s, served as the keynote speaker. In his address, Kiefer challenged Abilene Baptists: "Now is the time to work in these busy towns . . . The denomination that will be most faithful and self-sacrificing now, will likely be in front fifty years hence."[24] O.C. Pope followed Kiefer's statement with his own prediction for the future of First Baptist: "Abilene is destined to be one of our strongest churches."[25]

These statements proved prophetic. As Abilene grew, the members of First Baptist played key roles in the town's growth. In 1882, Otto W. Steffens moved his bank from Buffalo Gap to Abilene. In 1884, the bank became the First National Bank of Abilene, with First Baptist members Clabe Merchant as president and James Parramore on the board of directors. Another longtime member, George S. Anderson, became editor of the *Abilene Reporter News*. Anderson served as a deacon at First Baptist for more than seventy years.[26]

By the end of the nineteenth century, even more institutions and people came to the city. In 1900, the state government established a colony for the care of epileptics in Abilene. Originally directed by Dr. John Preston and later by Dr. T.B. Bass, the state-supported hospital soon changed its focus. Instead, the colony became the Abilene State School and served people suffering from various mental challenges.[27]

With Abilene rapidly becoming the "future great city of West Texas," as the founders had predicted, First Baptist Church used its mission projects to serve and shape the city. One of the earliest local mission efforts occurred in March 1885, when First Baptist created the Ladies Aid Society. The first women's organization in the church, the society held meetings for women and children. The group provided social activities and fellowship for the

Women's Convention, 1927

women of the church. Led by Mrs. George A. Pearce, the organization's first president, the society also undertook outreach projects, such as food and clothing drives for those in need in the area and beyond.[28] Furthermore, the members of the Ladies Aid Society worked to support First Baptist and undertook a fundraising campaign to pay off the last of the debt incurred by the construction of the inaugural church building.[29]

A third women's organization from First Baptist that served Abilene during the 1880s was the Mission Society. In 1889, all of the women's mission groups at the church combined to form the Baptist Women's Mission and Aid Society. The organization shortly after became one of the nation's first Women's Mission Union (WMU) chapters in the country. Through the WMU, the women of First Baptist played a significant role in the history of the church as well as the mission efforts to Abilene. The First Baptist women aided the church's preachers and their families, raised money and goods to help the less fortunate, and assisted state institutions like Buckner's Orphans Home with money, bedding, and clothing.[30]

First Baptist grew rapidly during the late 1800s and early 1900s, as did Abilene as a whole. The different groups within the church dedicated themselves to meeting the physical needs of First Baptist. At the same time, work to aid Abilene was a main focus of First Baptist. The dedication to building the community was present not just among the membership but also among the pastors.

Bennett Hatcher, the first permanent pastor, emphasized the need to assist children and young people. Members collected money to buy clothing for underprivileged Abilene youths, hoping that the recipients would feel pride in a nice set of clothes and, in turn, might be more inclined to attend Sunday school. Furthermore, a Children's Missionary Union began in order to focus the young people at First Baptist on mission activities. In 1890, the church established the Young People's Union Society with similar goals in mind. One of the first such organizations of its kind in the country, the society directly involved teenagers in the outreach of the church.[31]

Another theme of First Baptist's efforts to better serve Abilene appeared in the Sunday morning worship service. As the church grew, the membership possessed different ways of praising God. In order to embrace these differences while also offering celebration and worship of God, the church adapted its service to meet the varying skills of the membership. One example of changing worship practices occurred in 1889, when First Baptist organized its first official choir. Another example occurred in 1890, when questions arose over the use of cornets in worship. The church decided to try the brass instruments for three months before making a decision. After the trial period, an overwhelming majority of members chose to keep the horns as part of the service.[32] In 1901, the church began holding Sunday evening worship services, again as an attempt to meet the community's needs.[33]

Efforts to serve Abilene and the church were intertwined in the early years. In 1899, the women of First Baptist again helped raise money to meet a financial need in the church. When Pastor Lee Scarborough announced an urgent need of $50 for church expenses, the women's organizations held a "silver tea" in response. When the tea came to an end, the women had produced $53.[34]

The emphasis on helping Abilene never ceased at First Baptist, but in times of great crisis, the church focused more strongly on this area. When America entered World War I in 1917, outreach programs to the community dominated the attention of First Baptist. In response to President Woodrow

Rev. Millard Jenkens on steps of the second church building

Wilson's war message, male residents of Abilene formed Company I, 7th Regiment, 142nd Infantry, 36th National Guard Division. At Simmons College, the Student Army Training Corps, which included numerous students who attended First Baptist, prepared for war. Rupert N. Richardson, a young professor and member of First Baptist Church, led the Simmons College regiment.[35]

In April 1917, the government called up five thousand National Guardsmen from Abilene. Thousands more young men from Abilene and Taylor County joined the military before the war ended. The decline in the area's male population created considerable physical and emotional strain for local residents. The *Reporter News* kept Abilenians informed, regularly publishing letters from soldiers in training camps and local men fighting in Europe, as well as casualty lists.[36]

Many of the young men from Abilene who served during World War I were members of First Baptist. The church's pastor, Dr. Millard A. Jenkens, participated in the Camp Pastor Program and served for ten weeks as special camp pastor at Camp Cody in Deming, New Mexico. Jenkens's service ended when the Army canceled the program. First Baptist members thought that the soldiers needed religious support, and the church body sent a collective letter to T.P. Keppel, the third assistant secretary of war, in Washington. The letter stated:

> The First Baptist Church of Abilene, Texas, eleven hundred members, whose loyalty to the government in the fight for human freedom in the world is unquestionable, enters her most earnest plea for the full exercise of religious freedom for all faiths in this crucial hour and solemnly protests against the enforcement of the order eliminating the camp pastors from the Army camps.[37]

The congregation concluded the letter by saying:

> We voice the sentiments of nearly eight million Baptist citizens, who have contributed nearly half a million sons and are ready to give to the last dollar and the last man, who will feel they have been deprived of the exercise of their most sacred and God-given rights and the coveted opportunity to serve.[38]

Even though the Army refused to reinstate the camp pastor program, the members of First Baptist continued to fight for other issues they believed important to the war effort and their Christian ideals. In April 1917, the congregation sent a telegram to the president concerning prohibition: "We earnestly urge the immediate prohibition of the liquor by the National Government, as an emergency war measure to conserve the food supply, factory and farm production, and military efficiency."[39] As with the church's earlier letter to the government, the desired outcome failed to occur, although church members were able to take pride in knowing that they had taken a stand for their beliefs. Furthermore, the First Baptist appeal coincided with a growing national movement that culminated two years later with the passage of the Eighteenth Amendment to the Constitution, which established national prohibition.

The church's focus on serving Abilene continued in October 1918, when the Spanish flu infected Abilene. The disease created an international epidemic after the war. Some local people believed that the disease came to Abilene with a traveling circus; others said it arrived in the state aboard a German submarine hidden in the Gulf of Mexico as part of a plot against Texas. A shortage of doctors and nurses because of the war effort compounded the local fear of the flu. Numerous residents and organizations, including First Baptist and its members, worked to alleviate these fears and address the immediate issue of an epidemic.[40]

Girl's Auxiliary Coronation, 1954

The local Red Cross chapter formed a volunteer group to care for the afflicted. Members of First Baptist participated in these efforts. The Red Cross sent aides into people's homes to provide medical care. In the newspaper, a notice went out for all healthy women between the ages of eighteen and forty-five to volunteer to help. The Abilene Independent School District delayed the start of classes for two weeks, until the end of October, in an effort to reduce the spread of the disease. Furthermore, for two consecutive weeks in October, every church in Abilene closed in order to reduce chances of exposure. When the epidemic finally ended in 1919, 540,000 people had died in the United States. In Abilene, the death toll reached eighteen.[41]

As the world transitioned from the Great War to the 1920s, First Baptist adapted to meet the spiritual and physical needs of Abilenians. In 1918, the Women's Missionary and Aid Society reorganized itself to include all Baptist women in Abilene in an effort to maximize their reach into the city. The following year saw the beginning of the Girls' Auxiliary, which focused on introducing young women to mission work in Abilene and abroad.[42]

The strong support for mission work by the First Baptist congregation coming out of World War I reinvigorated efforts to help Abilene. As a result, First Baptist Church created several staff positions designed to organize and maximize mission work. Margaret Goodnight became the director of the Baptist Young People's Union. Also in 1920, E. Grady Hargrove became the superintendent of Christian education. Hargrove's title later changed to Educational Director. Having a minister whose job focused on directing the congregation's Christian education proved unique, with First Baptist the only church in the South to establish such a position at the time.[43]

Focusing on children and education allowed First Baptist to establish a foundation in the community and allowed for further outreach there. Vacation Bible School exemplified the missionary potential. First Baptist offered its first VBS program on June 11, 1928. Attending the inaugural event were 264 children. Many of these children attended First Baptist, but most went to no church, giving First Baptist members opportunities to minister to the spiritual and physical needs of children with no official connection to the congregation.[44]

Following the trend set during World War I, numerous community aid organizations appeared during the Great Depression of the 1930s. First Baptist facilitated its own relief and aid organizations, but the city, state, and national governments also established programs in which many members participated. At the local level, the Free Milk Fund provided free milk for Abilene children. The Sunshine Nursery and Negro Day Nursery sought to aid mothers with inexpensive child care while the parents looked for work. First Baptist members volunteered with all of these organizations, as well as with the New Deal agencies created by President Franklin Delano Roosevelt and Congress starting in 1933.[45]

First Baptist, in its own right, responded to the suffering caused by the Great Depression by increasing the church's missionary efforts and providing aid to those in need. These efforts further established the church as a prominent institution in Abilene. The aid work helped support community residents and thus helped Abilene survive a time of great economic distress.

In addition to assisting community members with physical needs during the crisis, the church also focused on prayer. In 1932, at the height of the Depression, the church held daily noontime prayer services where those present asked God to aid those in need, help America's leaders with their work, and help the country return to prosperity.[46]

Historians agree that although Roosevelt's New Deal measures, along with state and local assistance programs, helped to lessen the impact of the Great

Young people playing shuffleboard in the church basement, formerly used as the Soldiers' Center

Depression, it was another catastrophic event that brought the crisis to an end in the United States. World War II brought monumental changes to the nation, and Abilene was no exception.

During the early 1940s, the city experienced a dramatic increase in population when the Army established Camp Barkeley south of town as a training base. At its peak, the camp housed fifty thousand soldiers. The arrival of these personnel provided another outreach opportunity for First Baptist. When Camp Barkeley opened in 1941, First Baptist built and supported a chapel at the base. At the same time, the church's young women continually met to roll bandages for the Army's use in the war.[47]

The creation of a soldier center in the church basement, however, proved to be First Baptist's most significant mission effort for the Camp Barkeley troops. Church members converted the basement into a recreation center for servicemen. Officially named the Servicemen's Center, the church made the facility available to the troops on Friday and Saturday evenings and all day on Sundays. First Baptist dedicated the center in May 1943. Dr. A.C. Miller, the state supervisor of Baptist soldier work, served as the guest speaker. Although war rationing delayed the center's grand opening as First Baptist encountered difficulties acquiring furniture and carpet, the endeavor proved successful.[48]

The church offered troops a place for recreation and relaxation, with various opportunities for sports and games. On Sundays, the events followed a typical church format with doughnuts and coffee, Sunday school, Bible study, singing, and a worship service. During the week, the church opened the center at regularly scheduled times for soldiers to play games, read, and watch group entertainment. A buffet of dessert and snack items prepared by the women of First Baptist served as an enticement to come to the center. First Baptist and the Abilene community embraced these men, ministered to their unique needs, and provided an environment that blended recreation and relaxation with spiritual support and homemade sustenance.

The center was short-lived, closing at the end of the war with the government decommissioning of Camp Barkeley. Still, the mission's success remained indisputable. First Baptist reached more than fifteen thousand servicemen through the recreation facility.[49]

The ministry of First Baptist to the soldiers extended beyond the soldier center. During the war years, an average of 225 soldiers attended the church service each Sunday. Furthermore, since most of the soldiers were between eighteen and thirty years old and away from their families, First Baptist sought to ease the soldiers' homesickness. In 1943, an article appeared in the congregation's weekly newsletter urging all members to invite a soldier to dinner on Mothers' Day. The article stated, "There are thousands of boys in our midst who never spent a night away from home before being inducted."[50]

Just as prayer became a focus during the Great Depression, First Baptist members continued the practice during wartime. The church held a special prayer service for the men and women in military service on April 19, 1944. Four hundred sixty-one men and women from First Baptist served in World War II. At the prayer service, Pastor Jenkens asked members to pray "for our boys, and for a speedy end to the war, and for a just peace based on Christian principles." Those at the service also remembered America's leaders and "even our enemies."[51]

On June 6, 1944, First Baptist held another special prayer service for the Allied troops in Europe on the eve of the D-Day invasion of Normandy Beach in France. The invasion marked the largest effort of the war and served as the pivotal moment in the conflict that determined success or failure for the Al-

Young people in a prayer circle in the church basement

lies. The service began at 3:30 a.m. in Abilene, corresponding with the beginning of the invasion in France, and lasted until 8:00 p.m. Throughout the designated time, the church remained open, with members volunteering to cover the American soldiers and their allies with prayer. Members prayed for the safety and success of friends and relatives involved in the war, as well as the safety and success of thousands of people they never met. Later, when word came relaying the success of the operation, the prayers turned to thanksgiving to God for his faithfulness and protection.[52]

When World War II ended in 1945, First Baptist adapted its resources to meet the community's changing needs. Camp Barkeley closed, negating the need for a soldiers' center. The Women's Mission Union then converted the church basement into a nursery for the children of ministerial students at Hardin-Simmons. First Baptist also used the nursery for young children's Sunday school classes. Having classes for children from birth to age four allowed parents to attend Sunday school themselves.[53]

The relief-based mission undertakings of the church during the Depression and World War II increased First Baptist's focus on meeting the physical needs of Abilene. Beginning in the 1950s, First Baptist women's ministries maintained a clothes bank to help needy people in Abilene. The program re-

Mary Pender, Elwin Skiles, and Kitty Longacre pose with babies enrolled in the nursery program for Hardin-Simmons University students following World War II

ceived donations of used clothes from church members and then redistributed them. Giving clothes to those in need had been a practice throughout the history of First Baptist, but with the establishment of the clothing bank, it became an official ministry of the church.[54]

The loss of Camp Barkeley created some apprehension among Abilene leaders as roughly half of the town's population moved away with the closing of the base. These fears were abated when the federal government established Dyess Air Base in Abilene. The facility's construction caused the city's population to increase dramatically. From 1950 to 1960, the populace went from just over forty-five thousand to ninety thousand.[55] Enrollment in the Abilene Independent School District doubled, prompting school construction.[56]

With an increase in the number of families with young children and teenagers in Abilene, First Baptist members moved forward with an idea long in the minds of church leaders. The congregation desired the establishment

Young men playing basketball in the original church recreation building.

of a Christ-centered environment designed to promote Christian beliefs with the hopes of reducing juvenile delinquency in the city. This idea came to fruition in 1956, when members passed a resolution authorizing the purchase of the YMCA building west of the church building at a total cost of seventy thousand dollars. [57] For the next few years, the two organizations jointly used the building until the YMCA relocated to a new building on State Street.[58]

The use of the old YMCA building as a recreation building allowed First Baptist to use sports and games to minister to the community. The physical activities served as a point of contact with residents, and from there the church worked to meet physical and spiritual needs. The recreation ministry focused mainly on children, since the center's stated purpose was to provide a positive environment and an alternative to other activities that might lead to trouble. However, as First Baptist ministered to children, the actions furthered the opportunity to connect with parents and share the gospel of Jesus Christ. In 1957, First Baptist sponsored a basketball tournament for kids and divided them into age groups of "Juniors," "Intermediates," and "Young People." Sports proved successful at reaching the community. As a result, activities such as youth basketball leagues occurred annually at the recreation center.[59]

A television ministry cameraman films the Sunday morning service

First Baptist also sponsored events for adults designed to bring Christian men and women together in fellowship. The church regularly fielded men's softball and basketball teams in city leagues. In October 1957, First Baptist sponsored an adult men's bowling team that competed in a city-wide church league.[60]

In an effort to coordinate the recreation ministry in the best way, First Baptist established the position of recreation director. As a result, Hardin-Simmons University student Roy Harris was appointed director of the recreation building in December 1960. The following year, First Baptist members recognized this ministry's outreach potential and voted to recondition the recreation building to maximize the possibilities.[61]

In addition to providing recreational services to Abilene, the post-World War II era also brought technological updates to First Baptist. As television swept the nation in the 1950s, First Baptist decided to broadcast portions of the morning and evening services on an Abilene station. The initial broadcasts aired on February 15, 1954, from the newly dedicated sanctuary and marked the first televised worship service in Abilene's history.[62]

In 1957, First Baptist added another form of outreach by providing daily devotionals on local TV station KRBC-TV. At noon Mondays through Fridays, a five-minute devotional featured the church's pastor. On Sunday, the church continued to present a twenty-minute service that included a sermon and a performance by the choir.[63]

Interpreter for hearing impaired services

As a church with a mission focus, First Baptist continually received requests for assistance from area residents. In response, First Baptist members worked with other people and organizations in town. In 1957, for example, Maj. Cherb of the Abilene branch of the Salvation Army asked that First Baptist refer all transients to the Salvation Army for aid. Assistance provided included work at a dollar an hour. First Baptist agreed to work with the Salvation Army and help refer people.[64]

In 1959, First Baptist began another new ministry to take the message of Christ to a previously untapped segment of the community. In November of that year, a sign-language program started in the Sunday morning worship service to convey the message to hearing-impaired persons. Dr. Elwin Skiles, First Baptist's pastor, said in reference to the new ministry, "We have sent out invitations to many people who would benefit by such a ministry." Patsy Rivers, a Hardin-Simmons University student, served as the interpreter. She received assistance from Sammy Oates, another HSU student and football player who was hearing-impaired.[65] As of 2008, the ministry continued to be part of the worship service.

An interest in assisting community members with health issues remained part of the missionary spirit that guided First Baptist. In February 1960, First Baptist's Women's Missionary Union sponsored a clinic on Ambler Street to provide free medical aid to those in need, with a focus on children. The Ambler Baby Clinic, founded by Lula Mae Bond, the WMU community missions chairwoman, and Idus Owensby, the education director at First Baptist, involved several local doctors and specifically focused on low-income families connected to the Ambler Street Baptist Mission. Members from First Baptist and the Ambler Mission visited homes in the neighborhood to invite people to the clinic. The clinic began in a small frame house but later moved into the Ambler Mission. Local doctors S.J. Barron, George Dawson, Herman Schaffer, and Robert Lockhart worked at the clinic and examined patients at no charge.[66]

The clinic, originally intended to provide services to preschool-age children, expanded as the volunteer physicians examined older siblings on site. Medical professionals performed both well and sick examinations. By 1968, however, caregivers focused their efforts on sick-child care, as the Public Health Department associated with the city offered well-child exams and immunizations. The clinic's mission of providing free medical services for low-income families was significant because the only free medical care available in Abilene during the 1960s came from the county-supported clinic—care for which many of the people served by the Ambler clinic failed to qualify.[67]

Another area of outreach to young people in Abilene materialized through the establishment of a Boy Scout troop associated with First Baptist. The troop reflected First Baptist's interest in the development of programs for the younger men of the church body. D. Warren Craik served as chairman of the Boy Scout Troop 33 committee, recruiting ten-year-old boys enrolled in Sunday school. In letters to parents, Craik told them that the troop met at the church on Monday nights. He also expressed the goals and purpose of the troop. Craik wrote: "The development of our youth to be physically strong, mentally awake, and morally straight- to be citizens of character, with high spiritual ideals and motives is desirable and essential to our way of life."[68] Troop 33 proved successful, and three years later it renewed its charter with the national office of the Boy Scouts of America, listing twelve boys between the ages of eleven and fifteen as charter members.[69]

Rev. and Mrs. James Alexander hand out clothing from the First Baptist Clothes Bank

As the post-World War II era continued to reveal a changing social element nationwide, First Baptist remained committed to its mission of assisting the community in a time of growth and change. The church exhibited that commitment in a deacon's meeting in September 1963. The men discussed the national civil rights movement and the challenge to racial discrimination and subsequent events that had occurred the previous summer. Given the televised racial violence in cities throughout the South, especially in Birmingham, Alabama, and the success of the March on Washington, First Baptist leaders determined that it was time for a clear statement of the church's position on racial discrimination.

In one act, First Baptist officially condemned racial segregation. At the meeting, Jim Jennings, the chairman of the deacons, presented a resolution to go to the church body for a vote. The resolution stated, "Color will not be a determining factor for membership in the First Baptist Church." No segregation policy had ever existed at First Baptist, but in light of national events, church members wanted to clarify the issue and leave no question that the doors and the mission of the institution remained open.[70]

Also in 1963, First Baptist started another mission effort to serve the spiritual needs of the people of Abilene. Similar to the use of television in 1957, the church sponsored a daily sacred music program on a local radio station. The program reached ten thousand people daily by 1966. Titled "Inspiration," the fifteen-minute program aired on "KFMN stereo radio, 99.3 on your FM dial."[71]

Existing mission efforts in the community continued to grow throughout the last half of the twentieth century, further expanding the church's influence on the city. In 1964, the First Baptist clothing bank gave out more than two thousand articles of clothing to seventy families.[72] With an increased demand for aid from area residents, the clothing bank grew in size, operating out of rooms in the church basement. Reverend James Alexander, the former pastor at the Willow Street Mission, and his wife took over the clothes bank when they retired in 1955. The program ministered mainly to the Abilene community, but the Alexanders also sent boxes of clothes to people in need throughout the world. Further, by delivering clothes to people's homes, the Alexanders were able to look into other needs that the church might meet and to share the gospel of Jesus Christ as well.[73]

First Baptist continued to respond to national issues that affected people locally. In 1967, WMU members at First Baptist made one hundred Christmas bags for the Red Cross to send to American military forces in Vietnam. The following year, the WMU again made Christmas treat bags for men from First Baptist who were serving in the war.[74] On April 7, 1968, First Baptist hosted a city-wide, nondenominational memorial service for the murdered civil rights leader Dr. Martin Luther King, Jr. The service focused on King's life and sought to promote unity and community among Abilenians. The service involved clergy from seven local churches: Memorial Christian Church, Heavenly Rest Episcopal Church, John Knox Presbyterian Church, Antioch Methodist Church, First Baptist Church, Macedonian Baptist Church, and Sacred Heart Catholic Church.[75]

By 1968, First Baptist sought to refocus its mission work in Abilene to meet the changing needs of the community. The church hired Tom and Marilyn McMillan to conduct a study of the specific needs of Abilenians and then report to the church body. The McMillans, who were missionaries to Africa staying in a First Baptist mission home while on furlough, sent out a note to the First Baptist membership asking if anyone possessed an interest in mission work. Forty people responded and met with the McMillans at the church. The group then divided up and drove around town, taking notes on potential mission outreach programs. Upon returning to the church, the group compared notes, and Tom McMillan wrote his report.[76]

Numerous new outreach programs grew out of the report. For example, the church hosted suicide prevention groups and alcohol counseling. Call for Help, which began at First Baptist, helped people in Abilene find assistance

Rev. James Flamming

with a wide array of physical, financial, and emotional needs. The outreach project connected with the work influenced First Baptist's outreach programs for the next forty years.[77]

The renewed commitment and rejuvenation of home mission programs at First Baptist received tremendous support from the newest pastor, Dr. James Flamming. Flamming, familiar with McMillan's report, specifically addressed the changing role of First Baptist as part of the Abilene community. When First Baptist opened in 1888, its downtown location put it in the middle of the growing community. As Abilene grew, First Baptist built new missions and programs to serve the expanding community. By the beginning of the 1970s, though, the population had continued to move to the south, and most First Baptist members no longer lived near the building. As a result, Flamming addressed and redefined the role of First Baptist as a downtown church.

In 1969, Flamming shared his vision of First Baptist as a downtown church. He explained his view that churches throughout the country were struggling to redefine their role in diverse communities. For First Baptist Abilene, Flamming said, this definition involved its position as a "downtown" church.

First, according to Flamming, First Baptist needed to serve as "a bridge between what was and what is."[78] The church helped earlier generations through their problems, and it would provide the same assistance and comfort for current and future generations.

Second, Flamming wrote that as a downtown church, First Baptist should:

> reach out and minister to every segment of community: saved and lost, rich and poor, highly educated and less educated, those who live in walking distance and those who travel from afar, old and young, colored and white, strong and weak- all of these come under the umbrella of the ministry of a downtown church.[79]

Flamming added, "To neglect any of these elements is to neglect one's stewardship to Christ and the community."[80]

Furthermore, First Baptist possessed a unique responsibility to Hardin-Simmons University, Hendrick Memorial Hospital, and Hendrick Home for Children. While these institutions no longer relied solely upon First Baptist for support, the church's commitment to them had not changed since their founding. Flamming concluded his charge to the congregation by stating, "We are here in downtown Abilene for good reasons. Let us respond with mature courage to the above responsibilities."[81]

This inspirational call to action combined the missionary spirit of First Baptist's founders with a fresh understanding of present issues and future concerns. Therefore, First Baptist initiated several new outreach endeavors, including the hiring of Reverend Lester Vinson as associate pastor for missions and evangelism. A summer missions program also began in order to get the congregation's youth involved in mission work. The program included a wide range of volunteer activities in the Abilene community that allowed the young people in First Baptist to help groups such as the elderly and handicapped with simple home repairs, as well as working at different mission outreach programs.[82]

Following Flamming's commitment to reaching as many people in Abilene as possible, First Baptist reworked its television ministry and began a weekly live broadcast of the entire hour-long Sunday morning service in the 1970s. The idea for the new television ministry grew out of a survey sent to members in the spring of 1973. In the report to the church body, the Television Study Committee stated that members of First Baptist were interested in televising the 11:00 a.m. Sunday service. The committee further concluded that no other ministry was as effective at reaching the entire community. As a re-

Children and teachers participating in Vacation Bible School in the 1960s

sult, local TV station KTXS began broadcasting the Sunday morning worship service in 1974.[83]

The contract between First Baptist and KTXS called for the station to broadcast the service in color. First Baptist purchased the cameras and equipment, while KTXS furnished free air time and professionals to televise the program and take care of all camera upkeep. The two parties agreed to an eight-year contract.[84]

In November 1979, the contract expired, and the church examined the possibility of broadcasting on another station. KTAB, the local CBS affiliate, presented First Baptist with an offer, which the church accepted. The television ministry remained a successful outreach program, with viewership ranging between eleven thousand and eighteen thousand people each Sunday morning.[85]

Another new ministry focusing on the spiritual and physical needs of the congregation began in 1979. First Baptist purchased a building across the street for the Ministry of Counseling, and also looked into turning part of the building into a singles building. The idea was to provide single adults with a Christian environment in which to meet, socialize, and fellowship.[86]

Beginning in the 1980s, an official benevolence ministry existed at First Baptist. Run by the Benevolence Committee, the program sought to assist

Women participating in the First Baptist bus ministry, 1973

people with basic, daily needs and continued the church's history of physical assistance to Abilene. Several guidelines existed for providing assistance. People seeking assistance had to first contact Call for Help, a local clearinghouse agency that began at First Baptist and kept records on who asked for help, the type of assistance sought, and the frequency with which the person received aid. The program never gave cash. Furthermore, any request over $35 was referred to the Benevolence Committee before being granted. The aid given out by the Benevolence Program included transportation (such as bus tickets or gasoline vouchers), brown bag lunches, food vouchers, rent and utilities assistance, referrals to doctors for medical attention or to the Texas Employment Commission for jobs, counseling, and child care through the Abilene Day Nursery or the God's Little Ones center, the latter located at First Baptist.[87]

The Benevolence Program reached a substantial number of people in Abilene. In March 1980, for example, fifty people received aid totaling more than $230. During the next few decades, the ministry grew into other programs, such as the brown bag lunch program and, later, City Light Community Ministries.[88]

The Benevolence Program also allowed First Baptist to play a role in national and global issues. When a large number of refugees fled Cuba during

John Weeks, Mike Greenfield, and Bill Altom prepare brisket as part of the "Smokin' Grill Team" ministry (photo by Tiffany Fink)

the early 1980s, several migrated to Abilene. In 1981, the Benevolence Committee voted to assist nine Cuban refugees in Abilene with rent and groceries.[89]

First Baptist also remained committed to supporting local institutions. In 1981, the church participated in a community-wide drive to build a new chapel at the Abilene State School. First Baptist members donated more than thirty-five thousand dollars.[90]

The efforts to minister to the spiritual needs of Abilene continued throughout the end of the twentieth century. While the annual revivals at First Baptist ceased during the 1960s and 1970s, First Baptist still occasionally hosted revivals to spur on the people of the church and the community. On October 11-14, 1981, the church hosted "A Festival of Faith" at the Abilene Civic Center. The worship services connected to the festival attracted participants from throughout the community.[91]

The mission spirit of First Baptist and the recognition that the immediate mission field for the church was the one that lay just beyond the doors of the sanctuary continued to guide the efforts and personality of the institution. As the twenty-first century dawned, First Baptist carried on as an integral part of the Abilene community, ever searching and experimenting with new forms of outreach. For example, a catastrophic flood struck much of the city in July 2002. First Baptist members used a newly established outreach group called the Smokin' Grill Team to prepare and distribute meals to Abilenians as they cleaned and restored their homes. Another ministry team, Babies First, sought to connect with parents of newborns and meet physical needs while sharing the good news of the love of Jesus Christ.

These examples demonstrate a commitment on the part of First Baptist to love Christ and love others. In this case, the "others" were the residents of Abilene. For more than one hundred twenty-five years, First Baptist members endeavored to demonstrate their dedication to serving the community and reflected the heartfelt words of the hymn "They will know we are Christians by our love."

Chapter 2

"How Firm a Foundation"

Three important Abilene institutions rose from the foundation of mission work by First Baptist. Church members examined their community and felt called to meet the spiritual, educational, and physical needs of fellow residents. Through the ensuing mission work, First Baptist was instrumental in the establishment of a university, a hospital, and a home for children.

Less than a decade after the town's founding, several members of First Baptist Church expressed the desire for a Baptist college in Abilene. No institution of higher learning existed in West Texas at that time. The idea for a local college began with a group of Baptist men who gathered in Will Young's general store. The men believed that a college would serve the educational needs of their children while also promoting Christianity among Abilenians. From this small group, the idea spread.[92]

On August 2, 1890, Reverend G.W. Smith of First Baptist Church, along with congregants K.K. Legett and J.S. Williams, presented the idea of a Baptist college in West Texas to the Sweetwater Baptist Association. While many in the association agreed with the proposal, the sentiment was not unanimous. Rufus C. Burleson, the president of the largest and oldest Baptist college in Texas, Baylor University, stated that several previous attempts at founding colleges in West Texas had failed to materialize. West Texas Baptists needed to give all of their support to Baylor so that the existing school would succeed, he argued.[93]

Other than Burleson, however, no one else opposed the idea. With the majority of those present in favor of a college, the leaders of the Sweetwater

Baptist Association formed a committee to oversee the project. The committee asked for bids of land on which to build the new school. All members in the association's governing area, which stretched from Callahan County to El Paso County, received the opportunity to submit bids.[94]

The original reasons for establishing a Baptist college in Abilene supported the mission goals of First Baptist Church. As a result, the church leadership was already working on its proposal for Abilene as the home of the new college. The Sweetwater Association received only two bids, both from Abilenians. Henry Sayles, Sr. submitted a bid involving lots in the southern part of town. The other offer, which the association chose, came from a group of investors led by Otto W. Steffens, a local businessman and First Baptist member who owned the proposed land. The Steffens bid included a sixteen-acre plot two miles north of downtown Abilene, along with a gift of five thousand dollars to help with the construction of school buildings.[95]

The land given by Steffens for the college created a small sense of loss for the people of Abilene, especially for the early settlers. The establishment of the college meant that Abilenians lost access to a small, wooded area known as a habitat for wild turkeys. Unable to hunt the turkeys, some local residents found themselves without one of their established food sources, especially for holidays such as Christmas. Although this was not a significant problem, many of the early inhabitants never forgot the loss of their hunting privileges and often associated it with the college.[96]

The school's creation generated considerable excitement in Abilene's Baptist community. In the October 1890 minutes of the Missionary Society at First Baptist, a church member listed as Brother Wingo expressed the feelings of many in the church regarding what was then known as Abilene Baptist College. Wingo stated: "Resolved that we the First Baptist Church of Abilene gratefully accept and heartily endorse the work of the College Committee appointed by the Sweetwater Association and we hereby endorse the appointment of K.K. Legett, G.T. Harrington, Reverend G.W. Smith, Otto Steffens, and Henry Sayles as trustees to represent with plenary powers the First Baptist Church of Abilene."[97]

The laying of the cornerstone for the college's first building on July 4, 1891, was described as "a grand event for the ten-year-old Abilene."[98] According to Tommie Lou Clack, "It was such a party as we had never seen out here on the prairie land."[99] Special trains brought in people from all over the area. Many local residents of various religious affiliations marched in a parade from the downtown railway depot to the campus, led by Abilene's Fourth Regimental Band.[100]

At the ceremony, numerous people spoke, and the day's festivities culminated with the laying of the cornerstone. The picnic that followed was one of the most significant social events to date in Abilene history, with residents eating more than three tons of free beef. But two other aspects of the picnic provided the strongest memories for Clack.

One lasting impression involved men "firing an anvil" in celebration. This practice consisted of putting gunpowder in the indentation on top of the anvil, placing a second large piece of metal on top, and then lighting the gunpowder. According to Clack, "The resulting noise will frighten horses and cattle three miles away."[101] Another aspect of the celebrations proved even more memorable than loud explosions involving large pieces of metal: "The main thing I recall about the picnic was the ice. Simmons people had ordered a boxcar of ice shipped in on the Texas and Pacific Railroad. It was such a luxury, having all the ice you wanted on the Fourth of July."[102]

After the official founding of the college, the Board of Trustees set the school's first academic year to begin on September 13, 1892. A pamphlet circulated by the college announced the opening and outlined the college's mission: "The work of the college will be Christian education. Its founders have dedicated it to the promotion of Christian intelligence among the people of Texas and other states."[103]

However, Abilene Baptist College changed its name before the start of the academic term. The change resulted from a letter that G.W. Smith wrote to O.C. Pope in New York. Smith asked Pope to help find people who might be interested in assisting the school. Pope approached James B. Simmons, who also lived in New York. Simmons immediately sent five thousand dollars, a gift that allowed for the completion of the school's first building—a necessity for the opening of the college. When Simmons came to Abilene to visit the newly created college in September 1892, the trustees voted to change the name to Simmons College as a show of appreciation for his gift.[104] Simmons included one stipulation with his donation: "no religious test shall ever hinder any person . . . from entering and receiving instruction in said Simmons Col-

Hardin-Simmons University main entrance at Hickory Street (photo by Tiffany Fink)

lege."[105] Following this charge, Simmons College enrolled and taught all students, not just those belonging to the Baptist faith, thus expanding the outreach and effectiveness of the school.

First Baptist played a constant role in the life of the new college, ministering to the physical and spiritual needs of the students. During the first several years, the church's female members met to sew clothes and quilts for the young women attending Simmons College. Later, in early 1900, the congregation raised the money to build Anna Hall and Cowden Hall, which provided a much-needed increase in dormitory space for both male and female students.[106]

First Baptist provided another mission service for Simmons College in 1889. In that year, the Willing Workers Sunday school class raised $35 to have a fence built around the campus. Since Simmons College stood at the northern limits of Abilene, the fence served to keep cattle off of the grounds.[107]

First Baptist remained committed to serving the physical and spiritual well-being of the students at Simmons, a course of action that also ministered to Abilene as a whole. In 1905, Legett, along with Simmons College President

Charles Blaylock and several First Baptist members sew as part of a quilting group

Oscar Henry Cooper, founded the Simmons Bible Institute, a conference designed to promote religious study and learning. The annual event lasted for approximately ten days every January and attracted participants from all over the state. The topics of discussion ranged from religion and Christian living to the daily work of a preacher. The institute occurred as a joint venture with First Baptist Church. Daytime lectures took place at Simmons College, while First Baptist hosted the evening activities. First Baptist members also opened their homes as places for visitors to stay while in town for the Institute. The diverse presentations at the event exposed Abilenians to a wide array of Christian ideas, expanding the religious perspective of many residents.[108]

The efforts to minister to the physical needs of the Simmons students by First Baptist Church and its members included large building projects that also benefited local residents. In July 1902, the congregation voted to fund a waterworks system for Simmons College, which possessed no running water at the time. With the money approved by the church body, First Baptist created a new committee that undertook the installation of the pipes and the operation of the water system. The new system also served residents in

Baptist Young People's Union, 1914

the neighborhood adjacent to the campus, which was also without running water.[109] At the same time, the church collected money to build apartments for students and faculty, while First Baptist Pastor L.R. Scarborough took a leave of absence from his position to travel and raise money for the college.[110]

The efforts to assist Simmons College did not always involve something as large-scale as new buildings. The aid took many different forms and was a constant in the history of First Baptist. In 1909, the congregation purchased a pipe organ for the church sanctuary. The organ, "a two-manual instrument with 24 speaking stops," came from the M.P. Mollier Company, the largest organ factory in North America at the time. Simmons College organ professor C.H. Lewis, who also served as the organist for First Baptist, gave the dedicatory concert on the instrument on December 20, 1910. Fifty years later, when the church purchased a new organ, the original instrument became a gift to the college.[111]

In March 1914, First Baptist members collected $275.50 to provide scholarships to Simmons College students pursuing education and training as preachers. Two months later, a committee of church members lobbied the city government to pave Hickory Street from Simmons College to First Baptist. Members hoped that a newly paved road would ease transportation and encourage more Simmons students to attend First Baptist on Sundays. However, the city government failed to work at a pace pleasing to the congregation, and in February 1915 church members collected money to pay for the paving and undertook the operation themselves.[112]

The biggest support given by First Baptist to Simmons College over the years came through financial assistance. This monetary support allowed the college to survive and provide basic services to students. In 1915, First Baptist Pastor Millard Jenkens led deacons and other members in a vote to give a particular portion of First Baptist's annual budget to Simmons College. The annual donations to the school maintained the connection between the two institutions. Since Simmons students became a part of Abilene while pursuing their degrees, they also carried the ministry of First Baptist Church out into the community.[113]

Besides the annual donation from the First Baptist budget, the church also provided extra monetary and physical assistance to the school as needs arose. In March 1916, Dr. G.W. Truett, pastor of First Baptist Church of Dallas, wrote to First Baptist Abilene asking for financial aid in a statewide campaign to assist Baptist colleges in Texas. The Abilene congregation responded by giving assistance to Simmons College. The church raised twenty-three thousand dollars for the construction of Mary Frances Hall, a new dormitory that provided rooms for almost one hundred female students.[114]

The financial donations by First Baptist Church to the college addressed many different needs. In 1924, Simmons College sought to raise an endowment of five hundred thousand dollars, which would enable the college to achieve university status. Abilenians pledged two hundred thousand dollars, and the New York General Education Board—which not only had been instrumental in the founding of Simmons College but also was directed by James B. Simmons, the college's namesake—contributed one hundred thousand dollars. The school's students and faculty raised the final two hundred thousand dollars. The majority of the Abilenians, students, and faculty members who donated to the endowment fund were members of First Baptist. In that same year, the Women's Missionary Union at First Baptist created the Rosabel Breed

Logsden Chapel at Hardin-Simmons University (photo by Tiffany Fink)

Love Student Loan Fund to provide loans for students at Simmons College. The fundraising allowed First Baptist to serve the school and the community while also deepening the relationship between college and church.[115]

Many of the links between the university and the church came from individuals connected to both institutions. Judge and Mrs. C.M. Caldwell, members of the congregation, donated more than one hundred thousand dollars to Simmons College during the 1921-22 academic school year to build Caldwell Hall. The building, which opened in 1923, served as the home for the school's music department. In 1959, the Caldwell family again donated money for Caldwell Hall, this time to renovate the thirty-six-year-old structure, add a new wing to the building, and install air conditioning—a necessity for enduring West Texas summers.[116]

George Anderson, editor of the *Abilene Reporter News* during the first half of the twentieth century, was another individual connected to both Simmons University and First Baptist. Anderson supported the mission work of First Baptist to the university and the town. Anderson served as a trustee and benefactor to many local Baptist institutions. Anderson gave the university the money for Anderson Men's Dorm, providing the growing student body with more housing.[117]

First Baptist Church also used its facilities to support Simmons University as well as reach out to Abilene. The church opened its sanctuary to the university for the school's annual Lyceum series. In the Lyceum, prominent politicians, musicians, and speakers performed and lectured for the educational and spiritual benefit of Simmons students and the community. Through the series, the Abilene community experienced several talented people.

On February 24, 1924, former Polish Premier Ignance Jan Paderewski, the famed pianist, performed before an overflow crowd at First Baptist Church. Another internationally accomplished pianist, Serge Rachmaninoff, held a concert in First Baptist's sanctuary in 1933. Will Rogers, the popular cowboy humorist, entertained crowds at First Baptist on several occasions. The fact that such prominent artists came to a still-developing town in West Texas testified to the support that First Baptist provided to Simmons University and to the commitment that both institutions possessed to providing enlightening experiences to the Abilene community.[118]

The mission work of First Baptist and its members to Simmons University never waned, even during major crises such as the Great Depression. By providing physical support such as meals and clothes for students, as well as financial support, the church helped students continue their academic pursuits and allowed the university to remain operational through the economic calamity. First Baptist members also worked to acquire large monetary donations from prominent Texans. The most significant of these donations received by Simmons University during the 1930s came from John G. Hardin, a wealthy oil man from Burkburnett. The money given by Hardin was negotiated by several First Baptist members, including C.M. Caldwell, Rupert Richardson, and university President Jefferson Davis Sanderfer. The gift eventually totaled nine hundred thousand dollars and led the school to change its name to Hardin-Simmons University (HSU) as a show of gratitude to the Hardin family.

Richardson communicated the thoughtfulness with which university leaders decided upon the name change. He wrote that "if the voice of James B. Simmons could reach from the great beyond, we would hear: 'Change the name if it will insure the perpetuation of the institution, if need be, leave out the name of Simmons.'" Though the decision undoubtedly was a difficult one, university leaders felt it was for the good of the institution.[119]

University students Sunday school class

Through outreach programs and Sunday school classes, First Baptist ministered to the spiritual needs of the university students. During the summer of 1943, First Baptist organized the first city-wide Baptist Student Union (BSU) in Abilene. The church notified all the local colleges, not just Hardin-Simmons, concerning the organization, with seventy-five students responding. The students present attended Hardin-Simmons, Hendrick Memorial Hospital's nursing school, and Draushon's Business College, a local institution that taught skills such as typing and bookkeeping. The BSU offered students the opportunity to socialize with others from different schools while also participating in worship. The popularity of the BSU meeting led First Baptist to declare Mondays "Student Play Night" where the church could reach out to the college students.[120]

At times when First Baptist prospered financially, the church's support of Hardin-Simmons increased accordingly. In 1946, First Baptist voted to increase the budget allotment for HSU to eighteen hundred dollars to help with increasing expenses. Also in 1946, the church approved an additional donation of one hundred thousand dollars to the Greater Hardin-Simmons Building and Improvement Campaign, which sought to provide facilities for the growing student population.[121]

Elwin Skiles talking to HSU student Bonnie Bailey on the steps of the church sanctuary

First Baptist pastors maintained and encouraged the continual connection between the church and Hardin-Simmons. During Millard A. Jenkens's thirty-two-year tenure as preacher at First Baptist, he provided regular guidance to students, both those seeking advice on a career in the church as well as non-ministerial students who needed counsel.[122] Another pastor, Dr. Elwin Skiles, served First Baptist from 1952 to 1966. After leaving First Baptist, Skiles relocated several blocks north in Abilene and accepted the presidency of HSU, a tenure that lasted until 1977.[123] Dr. James Flamming, Skiles's successor at First Baptist, was the first HSU graduate to serve as pastor.[124]

The church's dedication to meeting the needs of Hardin- Simmons students brought about the creation of new programs directed at easing the fears and loneliness associated with going to college. Beginning in the 1950s, First Baptist started a program that connected HSU students with Abilene families. In the church newsletter, congregational leaders encouraged members to invite college students over for dinner. Similar to the World War II program for soldiers at Camp Barkeley, the adopt-a-student effort focused on the fact that many HSU students were away from home for the first time. First Baptist provided students with the opportunity to eat and connect with a local Christian family, a connection that reinforced the church's mission spirit by providing love and support for the students and that made the transition to college smoother.[125]

First Baptist's relationship with Hardin-Simmons also significantly influenced the physical look of Abilene. Members supported building projects like the Johnson Building and the Elwin L. Skiles Social Science Building. Efforts at ministering to the physical and spiritual needs of Hardin-Simmons took other forms as well. In 1961, HSU built Behrens Chapel-Auditorium and Theater. First Baptist donated its old organ, the Jenkens Memorial Organ, for use in the new auditorium.[126]

First Baptist never faltered in its dedication to supporting Christian higher education in Abilene. The church maintained a constant role in the life of Hardin-Simmons. The church annually presented students with scholarships, operated a university ministry, and sponsored social events and mission trips. The dedication of First Baptist to Hardin-Simmons allowed the church to minister to thousands of young people over the years while also providing a major institution for Abilene.

The second major Abilene institution founded by First Baptist Church that sought to meet the community's physical needs was West Texas Baptist Sanitarium. Millard Jenkens first mentioned the idea of a modern, church-supported hospital in Abilene in 1918.[127] In 1921, the Simmons University trustees took Jenkens's idea and developed the plan for a Baptist hospital in West Texas.

The Abilene Emergency Hospital already was in existence, but the building was an old two-story frame house at South Fourth and Sycamore streets that did not have enough rooms or equipment to meet the city's needs.[128] The Simmons trustees believed that Abilene needed a top medical facility, and they assembled a committee to raise the necessary money and build the hospital. First Baptist remained involved in the process, especially since the majority of the committee members attended First Baptist.[129]

The committee appealed to all the area Baptist congregations for funds. First Baptist Church Abilene took the lead in the mission opportunity, donating the most money of the churches involved. The proposed cost of the hospital came to $113,210. Jenkens led the fundraising campaign. By 1923, the committee had received ninety-two thousand dollars. With the majority of the money collected, construction began on a five-story, seventy-two-room building. On September 15, 1924, West Texas Baptist Sanitarium officially opened just south of Simmons University on a site donated by C.M. Caldwell.[130]

Jenkens expressed his delight over the dedication, stating, "For three years we dreamed, prayed, talked hospital, but the signs of promising interest did not develop rapidly." Jenkens went on to say: "Finally, the sick and suffering in Abilene needing the strong helping hand of a hospital and the conviction of the community and Baptist brotherhood to fulfill the call of a healing ministry . . . led to the opening of the West Texas Baptist Sanitarium, a Christian hospital."[131]

The new hospital provided West Texas with one of the best options for health care in an area that stretched from Fort Worth to El Paso. At the same time, West Texas Baptist Sanitarium gave First Baptist another way to minister to the community's physical and spiritual needs. All patients received treatment at the hospital, regardless of religious affiliation or ability to pay. Through the work of the hospital, First Baptist helped those suffering in the community, while also exhibiting Christian love to all.

West Texas Baptist Sanitarium immediately established itself as a vital part of the community. During its first year of operation, the hospital admitted more than eight hundred patients. As with the Simmons University, First Baptist included money for the hospital in the church's annual budget. As well as the annual donation from the church, First Baptist also regularly sup-

Hendrick Medical Center (photo by Tiffany Fink)

ported the hospital in other ways. Every Mother's Day, First Baptist held an offering for the hospital. The money served as a benevolence fund that allowed patients without means to receive medical services.[132]

The Mother's Day Charity Fund was the first of its kind among churches in the United States, and a substantial success. In 1953 alone, 715 charity cases received aid through the benevolence program. In 1956, the hospital gave out more than seventy thousand dollars in free medical services. As a result of the success, by the 1950s, churches in every state with a Baptist hospital started similar funds.[133]

The Mother's Day offering lasted for more than twenty years. In addition to raising money for the hospital, the ceremony involved with the offering reaffirmed the mission relationship between First Baptist and the West Texas Baptist Sanitarium. Beginning several weeks before Mother's Day, the church newsletter continually reminded the membership of the upcoming offering. First Baptist also published inspiring stories of people helped by the benevolence program. The Sunday morning service on Mother's Day also included lots of ceremony designed to emphasize the mission work of First Baptist through the hospital. In 1943, for example, hospital director E.M. Collier presented the institution's needs to the church body during the morning worship service. After the deacons collected the offering, they presented the money to Collier in a large basket in front of the congregation.[134]

First Baptist's relationship with West Texas Baptist Sanitarium remained constant over the years, even in difficult economic times. By 1935, the hospital found itself in a desperate financial situation. The Great Depression created cash shortages nationwide. In West Texas, people seeking medical assistance found themselves unable to pay their hospital bills and reliant on the benevolence fund. West Texas Baptist Sanitarium served a mainly rural area. The directors understood the financial restrains placed on the community; as the hospital stayed true to its call to provide health care for all West Texans, the directors agreed to allow patients to pay for medical services in whatever way proved most feasible. Since many of the patients were farmers, payment often involved eggs, crops, or livestock instead of money.[135] As word about the policy spread, the number of charity cases increased.

The lack of financial resources created other problems for West Texas Baptist Sanitarium. It became difficult to hire enough people to cover all of the jobs necessary to maintain the institution. In the face of a staffing shortage and a budget crunch, hospital personnel took on extra duties to keep West Texas Baptist Sanitarium running. Employees worked their regular shifts as doctors, nurses, and administrators and then helped with cleaning duties. Staff members also worked in the kitchen, performing jobs like shelling peas. To compensate employees for the extra work and low wages, the hospital provided free meals in its cafeteria.[136]

The staff's dedication to their mission and the commitment of Abilenians to the hospital were exemplified in an episode involving black-eyed peas. In the summer of 1935, local farmers produced a bumper crop of the vegetable. Word soon spread throughout the community that the hospital would accept peas as payment, and people brought in their produce to cover medical bills. At the same time, area residents learned that the hospital was experiencing a food shortage. Farmers responded by donating their extra black-eyed peas to the hospital to be used as food for patients. As a result, the hospital collected such huge quantities of peas that everyone connected with the institution—doctors, nurses, even hospital director E.M. Collier—spent all of their free time shelling peas. The black-eyed peas provided the main food item in the hospital cafeteria for both patients and staff, serving as the staple of many people's diets. Collier recalled, "I don't think we would have survived without someone thinking to give us that first bushel of peas . . . and then the bushels just kept coming."[137]

Statue dedicated to the mission of Hendrick Medical Center (photo by Tiffany Fink)

During the Depression, the financial support from First Baptist and other local churches was not always adequate to meet all of the hospital's expenses. The number of charity cases increased, which sharply strained the benevolence program. The hospital found paying its bills more difficult without a steady supply of cash. In 1932, for example, West Texas Baptist Sanitarium met its mortgage payment only after sending out an urgent appeal to the local churches describing the dire situation. In 1935, the same problem arose.[138] With First Baptist Church members also suffering from the effects of the Great Depression, the call for aid failed to bring in enough money to meet the hospital's bills. As a result, West Texas Baptist Sanitarium was threatened with closure.

In response to the serious financial situation, E.M. Collier, the hospital's director, approached Thomas G. Hendrick for help.[139] Hendrick, a former rancher and judge from Odessa, had made a fortune in the oil business. In 1932, he and his wife, Ida, retired and moved to a ranch in Shackelford. Because of their advanced years and health concerns, the Hendricks soon moved again, this time forty miles south to Abilene. While in Abilene, the two attended First Baptist Church.[140]

Collier sent word to Hendrick that the hospital needed aid. Hendrick soon called Collier to come to Hendrick's office and talk. The hospital needed slightly less than forty thousand dollars to pay all its debts. Collier planned to ask for only that amount. But when Hendrick asked what the institution needed, Collier surprised himself by replying that the hospital needed forty thousand dollars for its debts and another hundred thousand dollars for a new wing to better serve Abilene and the surrounding area.[141]

The request shocked Hendrick—he slapped his hands on his desk so hard that his chair rolled across the floor, striking the wall and tipping backwards, depositing the seventy-three-year-old man onto the floor. Collier also expressed shock at the amount that he asked for but later believed that the Lord guided his words.[142]

Hendrick told Collier that he needed to think about the request. After Collier left, Ida Hendrick told Thomas that she needed to talk to him about "that nice young man from the sanitarium."[143] Ida reminded her husband of a promise he once made to God. At a cowboy camp meeting, a preacher asked the listeners what work God had performed in their lives. Thomas Hendrick stated that he felt blessed by the Lord and that if possible he would do good works in the future to glorify God. Ida informed her husband that the time to perform those good works had arrived. The next morning, Hendrick called Collier and said, "Alright young man, I'm ready to build if you are." One year later (at the urging of Collier and C.M. Caldwell), the hospital board and the Baptist General Convention of Texas voted to rename the sanitarium "Hendrick Memorial Hospital." [144]

Over the years, Hendrick Memorial grew to meet the medical needs of Abilene, and First Baptist continued to support the hospital. During World War II, Hendrick Hospital expanded its physical plant to accommodate the local population increase brought on by the construction of Camp Barkeley. To build a new wing to serve the growing populace, the hospital received a wartime emergency grant from the federal government as well as local support through First Baptist.[145]

First Baptist's loyalty to Hendrick Memorial was not just financial. The church recognized the hospital as a means of outreach to the community. In 1958, the First Baptist WMU founded the Hendrick Hospital Auxiliary, a program designed to make the hospital stay of the patients easier. A group of

Verna Lee Hill & Leona Wetsel volunteer with the Hendrick Auxiliary

First Baptist women including Agnes Beckham, Hazel Lewis, Verna Lee Carson Hill, and Maewyn Herring went to E.M. Collier and asked about starting an auxiliary. Collier agreed, and a Mrs. Woodram, who organized the mail for the hospital, served as the director. Through the auxiliary, volunteers delivered the mail, organized a gift shop, and provided books and magazine for patients. Through the work of WMU members and other volunteers, the auxiliary expanded over the years to provide a wide range of assistance services, including providing videos for patients and operating visitor information centers. Hundreds of First Baptist members worked to assist area families during the most difficult of situations.[146]

Over the years, Hendrick continued to grow. By 2008, First Baptist no longer served as the hospital's main financial supporter. However, the church continued to give an annual portion of its budget to the hospital. When the hospital constructed new buildings to meet the changing needs of West Texas, First Baptist and its members played prominent roles. New facilities like the Hendrick Children's Hospital and the Vera West Women's Center expanded the institution's importance in Abilene and extended the mission work of First Baptist in the community.

The mission outreach of First Baptist Church also played a prominent role in the creation of a third significant Abilene institution: Hendrick Home for Children. First Baptist acted less directly in the establishment of the children's home than in the hospital and college. Still, First Baptist proved significant in the home's history, thus presenting the church with another venue for shaping Abilene's history while ministering to specific needs in West Texas.

When Thomas and Ida Hendrick drew up their will in 1936, they made provisions to leave a considerable portion of their fortune to establish and run a home for children. The total amount of money in the trust fund exceeded 1.5 million dollars.[147] Not intending to establish an orphanage or hospital, the Hendricks wanted their institution to provide a permanent home for healthy children in need. To carry out the plan, Thomas Hendrick purchased fifty-two acres on the southeastern edge of Abilene. In 1939, contractors completed work on the Hendrick Home for Children.[148]

The first twelve children arrived on June 22, 1939.[149] Most of the early children came from rural areas as victims of the Great Depression. The move from the country to Abilene, combined with separation from family members, caused difficult emotional times for the children. In addition, most understood little about the financial situation of their families.[150]

Even though the Hendricks attended First Baptist, the residents of the home were under no mandate to attend the church. Church attendance was mandatory, however, with residents choosing among First Presbyterian, First Baptist, and St. Paul's Methodist. If children had no previous religious affiliation or preference, they attended First Baptist.[151] As a result, numerous residents of Hendrick Home received services from First Baptist. First Baptist also used its connection to the children's home to minister to the residents.

The story of Gloria, Carl, and Ray Trusler offers an example of the situations that brought children to Hendrick Home. In 1954, Barbara Trusler, the children's mother, contracted polio while going through a divorce. Paralyzed in a Fort Worth hospital, Trusler found herself unable to provide for her children. A relative in the Abilene area contacted Hendrick Home director Tom Roberts and explained the family's plight. Roberts admitted all three children. Barbara Trusler later stated, "I don't think I could have ever come back from polio had I not known that my children were being cared for."[152]

Over the years, the directors of Hendrick Home for Children widened the institution's services. A Family Aid Program began in 1968, providing assistance to children while they lived in their own homes instead of moving to the Hendrick facilities. As a result, more than six hundred children in two hundred fifty-eight homes received aid. In 1978, Hendrick Home opened its Emergency Group Home at the request of the Texas Department of Human Resources. Located on North Third Street, this facility served an eleven-

Hendrick Home for Children (photo by Rob Fink)

county area and provided temporary care for children in crisis, abused children, and children whose home life had become disrupted.[153]

In 1971, Hendrick Home underwent expansion and remodeling. Buildings were added, including a gym and a heated swimming pool. The remodeling changed the dormitory format of the living areas into apartment-style rooms for the children.[154]

The expansion of the facilities and outreach programs at Hendrick Home over the years allowed the institution to better serve the Abilene community while also changing with the needs of society. By 2008, Hendrick Home housed fifty children, with most living in family-style cottages on the Hendrick campus. Furthermore, a family care program provided assistance for single parents and helped their families achieve financial, emotional, and spiritual stability. Education constituted a major component of the family care program, with parents working on advanced degrees while living at the Hendrick Home facility.[155]

First Baptist continued to assist Hendrick Home throughout the institution's history. The church provided emotional and physical support as the church home of numerous children. Through its support of Hendrick Home, First Baptist served West Texas.

The emphasis of First Baptist and its members on meeting Abilene's needs played a dramatic role in the area's history. Church members believed in their community. Through this support, First Baptist pursued improvements in higher education, health care, and care for children, a firm foundation of services to the growing community.

Chapter 3

"Bringing in the Sheaves"

First Baptist greatly influenced the development of Abilene in terms of key service institutions, but the church also ministered to the community's spiritual needs by creating mission churches throughout the town as the settlement continued to grow and thrive. The members of the church again followed Jesus Christ's Great Commission, literally taking the message to the people of Abilene.

The founders of First Baptist Church chose to name their institution as such with great hopes that theirs would be the first of many Baptist congregations in the community. The deeply held conviction that the church and the settlement must grow was evidenced by the commitment to developing missions throughout the city. As Abilene expanded and the population increased, First Baptist responded by extending missions into newly populated areas. The efforts produced significant results.

Many of the Baptist churches throughout the city grew out of First Baptist's missionary spirit. Church leaders held fast to the belief that theirs need not be the only Baptist church in town, but rather the first of many. The importance of people taking Jesus Christ as their Savior and becoming involved in a church superseded any desire that First Baptist's own membership or attendance grow. The belief that more Baptist congregations would exist in Abilene was evident in the name selected by the founders of First Baptist. In choosing "First Baptist Church of Abilene" instead of "Abilene Baptist Church," the charter members expressed the expectation that their denom-

The First Baptist congregation on the front steps of the 1910 church building

ination would spread throughout the city. As it turned out, the majority of Baptist churches that eventually formed in Abilene were directly related to First Baptist's mission efforts.

With these goals in mind, the church launched its first city mission early in Abilene's history. On April 10, 1892, Pastor R.T. Hanks led First Baptist members in the establishment of a Sunday school at the Hayes Laundry Building on Oak Street. Known as both the Oak Street Mission and the Southside Mission Chapel, the mission ministered to those living on the southeastern edge of the settlement.[156]

First Baptist's members volunteered at the mission, providing for any needs that arose. In 1896, a severe storm hit Abilene, damaging the First Baptist Church building and the Southside Mission Chapel. The Ladies Aid Society from First Baptist handled the repairs to the mission. The women raised money, collected supplies, and supervised the repair work.[157]

First Baptist pastors led the missionary efforts within the city. Pastor Lee Scarborough possessed a strong passion for mission-oriented projects. In

Calvary Baptist Church (photo by Tiffany Fink)

1906, First Baptist started another mission Sunday school, this time in the Valley View neighborhood. This mission later became Calvary Baptist Church. At the same time, First Baptist purchased a lot for yet another new mission across the street from the downtown fire station.[158]

As First Baptist established missions, church leaders expected the missions to eventually become independent. With the support of First Baptist, the Southside Mission Chapel moved to establish itself as an independent institution. In 1907, the mission purchased land on Oak Street, built a church building, and changed its name to Oak Street Baptist Church. One year after establishing itself as its own church, Oak Street Baptist officially changed its name to Southside Baptist Church.[159]

The focus on meeting Abilene's spiritual needs led First Baptist to remain open and available to assist new congregations begun by other groups. North Park Baptist Church's founders settled at the northern edge of town with the goal of extending ministry and outreach to the students at Simmons College. This church, which became College Heights Baptist Church and then University Baptist Church, received financial assistance from First Baptist as the congregation constructed its church building in 1908. Additionally, the women of First Baptist helped the new church to establish its own Women's Mission Union chapter.[160]

Southside Baptist Church (photo by Tiffany Fink)

As Abilene's population grew and the city expanded, First Baptist built more missions to serve the new neighborhoods. In 1908, First Baptist members began another a mission Sunday school on Walnut Street that served the northeast portion of town. To better help the Walnut Street Mission reach those in its neighborhood, First Baptist also paid to build a chapel at the mission site.[161]

Following the pattern established by the Southside Mission, the Walnut Street Mission became an independent church in September 1921. Walnut Street Baptist Church operated in the original mission chapel. The building and lot, however, still belonged to First Baptist. First Baptist allowed Walnut Street Baptist to use the facility for free until the new congregation raised the funds to purchase the building.

The friendship between the two churches continued when, three years later, a fire destroyed the Walnut Street building. Since First Baptist still owned the structure and also had insurance on the property, the First Baptist congregation voted in favor of using the insurance money to construct new facilities for Walnut Street Baptist Church.[162] The new church later moved to a site at North Thirteenth and Cypress streets. The church changed its name in conjunction with the move and became Immanuel Baptist Church.[163]

First Baptist sought to reach all people in Abilene through mission building projects. The institution opened a mission in north Abilene to minister to the city's Hispanic population in the early 1900s. The mission grew from the work of Jentry Holmes, a student at Simmons College. Holmes conducted

University Baptist Church (photo by Tiffany Fink)

Primera Iglesia Bautista (photo by Tiffany Fink)

home visitations within the community. When Millard Jenkens learned of Holmes's work, the pastor requested that First Baptist purchase a lot, build a home for Holmes, and start a mission to further his work. This effort became the Mexican Baptist Mission. After World War I, a pastor known as

Elmwood Baptist Church (photo by Tiffany Fink))

Brother Bejarano took over the mission, whose congregation grew to exceed the capacity at the original location. First Baptist located and purchased a new site and funded the construction of facilities to accommodate the church's increased membership. In 1951, the mission became an independent entity known as the First Mexican Baptist Church.[164]

The emphasis on building missions in Abilene remained a significant aspect of First Baptist's focus, regardless of the passage of time and significant world events. Despite the financial hardships felt by local residents, First Baptist Church continued its mission work during the Great Depression. In 1931, the Sunset Mission opened at 3318 South Third Street. Seventy-four people attended the first service, and Millard Jenkens delivered the inaugural sermon. In 1935, the mission became Sunset Baptist Church and in 1965 changed its name to Elmwood Baptist Church.[165] In 1938, the Women's Missionary Union began a mission at the Abilene Brick Plant to serve workers and their families. The mission closed in 1942.[166]

The efforts at supporting mission work in Abilene during the Great Depression also came from individuals in the church. Philanthropic members Thomas and Ida Hendrick donated cloth and other materials to First Baptist. Each summer, the church distributed the cloth to its various missions in Abilene so that women of the different Baptist institutions could sew clothes for neighborhood children for the upcoming school year. At Christmas and Thanksgiving, the Hendricks purchased turkeys and other food items for gift baskets that were distributed throughout the community. The local Baptist mission churches, as well as First Baptist, annually gave the Hendricks the names of local families who received the baskets.[167]

One prominent Depression-era mission that benefited from the aid of the Hendricks, as well as other First Baptist members, was the Friendship Mission. Started by First Baptist, this mission began in southeast Abilene in 1938. At the time, this area had no church or mission and possessed a reputation for vandalism and other problems involving neighborhood children. Located at South Sixth and Willow streets, the Friendship Mission, also known as the Willow Street Mission, sought to help redirect neighborhood children into positive activities with a Sunday school, a Boy Scout troop, and social and recreational programs. First Baptist member James Alexander and his wife moved to supervise the new mission, and fifty-four people joined as charter members.[168]

The effort at the Friendship Mission proved a success. The first year alone saw three hundred conversions and baptisms. Several programs began that met the spiritual and physical needs of the neighborhood and attracted hundreds of people to the mission. Some of the programs included a sewing room and a public health dispensary. The membership of the Friendship Mission grew so large by 1946 that First Baptist purchased an old chapel from Camp Barkeley to serve as the mission's building. First Baptist members then moved the structure from the decommissioned Army base south of town to the building's new location at South Eighth and Pecan streets.[169]

First Baptist opened the Cherry Street Mission in February 1949. This mission existed in the same neighborhood as the Friendship Mission and found itself competing to serve the same people and doing the same work. In order to economize its efforts, the Cherry Street Mission united with the Friendship Mission in 1953, when the latter become an independent church. The new congregation took the name Friendship Baptist Church.[170]

Even after Friendship Baptist became an independent institution, the church stayed connected to First Baptist. Throughout 1976, Friendship Baptist assumed a satellite affiliation with the older congregation. The year-long relationship connected the leadership and membership of the two churches. As part of the arrangement, Friendship Baptist and First Baptist coordinated programs and projects to reach a wider constituency in Abilene while promoting the connection between the two churches. Finally, the agreement allowed the larger and more financially secure First Baptist to assist Friendship with budget-related concerns. Each institution maintained its autonomy, and the agreement asserted: "This satellite relation is assumed in the firm conviction that God will be honored and both congregations will be mutually strengthened in the work of the Lord."[171]

Beginning in the 1950s, as with the other mission programs of the church, First Baptist focused on methods by which to carry on outreach programs while evolving with the changing social climate within the community. In 1952, many of Abilene's Baptist churches pooled their mission-building efforts and established the City Baptist Mission Board. The community-wide work of the board led First Baptist to coordinate its efforts with those of other churches. Even with its work as part of the City Baptist Mission Board, however, First Baptist continued to establish other missions and churches independent of the collaborative efforts in the city.[172]

The belief that all Abilenians should be exposed to the message of Jesus Christ's love remained the driving force behind First Baptist's mission projects. Throughout the last half of the twentieth century, the city expanded its boundaries to the south and west. In response to the city's changing demographics, First Baptist sponsored a mission in the new neighborhood of Elmwood West in 1953.

First Baptist members circulated a flier throughout the neighborhood that detailed the plans for the new church. Titled "Coming to Elmwood West...," the leaflet advertised a "new Baptist church located at 7th and Buccaneer; Sponsored by the Baptist Churches of Abilene, co-operating with the Southern Baptist Convention which embraces 28,000 churches and over 8,000,000 members."[173] First Baptist estimated the initial cost of establishing the church at about twenty-five thousand dollars. Reverend S.B. Hughes received the call as pastor-builder. Hughes had connections with the Department of City Missions of the Baptist General Convention of Texas and thus brought leadership and experience as the supervisor of construction. Even while the construction was going on, the leaders in the new mission church began Sunday school, a training union, and regular preaching services in temporary housing near the building site.[174]

The groundbreaking for the Elmwood West Mission occurred at the end of April 1954. Support for the new mission proved so strong that on May 2, Hughes held the first services even though the mission did not possess a building yet. Worshipers met in Bonham Elementary School, directly adjacent to the mission's lot.[175]

Pioneer Drive Baptist Church (photo by Tiffany Fink)

The First Baptist membership actively supported the efforts of the new mission. First Baptist Pastor Elwin Skiles urged his congregants to take part in the work of the Elmwood West Mission. In the "Pastor's Paragraphs" feature in the church newsletter, Skiles expressed his support for the new church: "We encourage members who live in the Elmwood West area to give prayerful consideration to this new Baptist work. In this extension of our church you will find marvelous opportunities for service and fellowship."[176]

One hundred nine members from First Baptist decided to serve as founders of the Elmwood West Mission. The new mission church grew so rapidly that within two years of its establishment, the church became independent, taking the name Pioneer Drive Baptist Church.[177] As with the other mission churches begun by First Baptist, Pioneer Drive continued to grow and prosper over the years, further advancing the Baptist cause in the community.

Under the leadership of Dr. Skiles, First Baptist organized yet another mission church in 1951, this time in the Sears Addition in north Abilene. The Ambler Avenue Baptist Mission built upon the work of the older First Mexican Baptist Church, seeking to minister to the Spanish-speaking community

Lakeside Mission

in Abilene. Interest in the mission came from a group of Hardin-Simmons students, led by Sallie Moore, who volunteered in the neighborhood and felt the need for more outreach in the community.[178]

First Baptist also continued to participate in mission work in conjunction with other Baptist churches in town. Two years after First Baptist began the Ambler Mission, the church helped the Abilene Baptist Association establish the Lakeside Mission at Fort Phantom Lake. Although this mission was technically under the association's support, First Baptist ran the mission and funded it through the church's annual budget. When needs arose, First Baptist addressed them. For example, in 1960 the Lakeside Mission needed a new rug. In response, the First Baptist newsletter put out a call for a donation; not long afterward, a slightly used rug arrived at the mission.[179]

Not all of First Baptist's mission efforts lasted. Abilene expanded very slowly to the north, and as a result the Lakeside Mission closed in 1962 because of low attendance. Other mission projects prospered, though. The Crescent Heights Mission, organized in 1954, later became Crescent Heights Baptist Church. The Ambler Avenue Baptist Mission grew throughout the 1950s and 1960s. All the while, First Baptist continued to help the independent Baptist churches in town whenever needs arose. In 1963, the First Mexican Baptist Church moved into a new building. Two First Baptist members, Mrs. B.A. Duffy and her daughter Mrs. Howard Wilkins, paid for the building's construction.[180]

Using the missions to minister to the spiritual needs of Abilenians allowed First Baptist to establish points of contact, learn of further unmet needs, and

Crescent Heights Baptist Church (photo by Tiffany Fink)

Ambler Avenue Baptist Church

address those concerns. On March 1, 1964, the Missions Committee at First Baptist established a preschool for Spanish-speaking children at the Ambler Mission. The idea came from First Baptist member Herman Petty. The purpose of the school was to acquaint children with English and thereby prepare them for immersion in the city's public school system. Since many came from predominantly Spanish-speaking families, these children were at a severe disadvantage when thrust into the public school system in Texas, which

Lytle South Baptist Church (photo by Tiffany Fink)

at the time required that all instruction be given in English. Through the preschool, the children received a foundation that enabled them to succeed in school, and First Baptist members met a significant need in the community.[181]

When First Baptist commissioned Tom McMillan to study the church's mission opportunities in 1968, he discussed the work at the Ambler Mission. McMillan reported that the mission's members wanted to undertake more of the leadership in their own church. McMillan set a goal for the Ambler Mission of self-support by January 1974. The plan called for the mission to take on half of its budget and then increase this by ten percent a year until the mission was responsible for its entire budget. McMillan also called for the construction of more Sunday school and auditorium space at the Ambler Mission. Following the advice of the report, the mission elected its first deacons and became an independent church on November 24, 1974.[182]

The work to establish missions to serve Abilene continued throughout the end of the twentieth century. Under the pastorship of Bill Brewster, First Baptist established five mission churches during the 1980s and 1990s. The La Bautista El Camino Mission opened in the 1980s and became an independ-

Templo Bautista Church (photo by Tiffany Fink)

ent church in 1987. The Ash Street Mission and the Quail Valley Mission began in 1987 and 1988, respectively. Both also later became independent.[183]

In 1988, First Baptist established the Lytle South Mission, which later became Lytle South Baptist Church. First Baptist and the missions committee worked for three years before the official groundbreaking for the mission facility took place on July 24, 1988. Seventy-five people attended. Construction on the mission lasted for five months. On October 26, 1988, thirty people attended the steeple-raising ceremony at the partially completed building. Those in attendance took part in a short devotional before receiving coffee and a tour of the unfinished building. The mission's first service, led by Pastor Rodney Watson, occurred on December 11, 1988. Watson stated that the new church existed to provide a "warm, informal atmosphere where families are strengthened, friendships are established, and spiritual needs are met."[184]

In 1990, First Baptist established the Hispanic Mission, which later changed its name to Templo Bautista Iglesia. Located at South Eleventh and Sycamore streets, the mission served a neighborhood south of the T&P Railroad. The mission encouraged neighborhood families to participate in pro-

Abilene Baptist Social Ministries

grams such as Vacation Bible School. The location doubled as the site of Abilene Baptist Association Social Ministries, which housed a pantry available to any members of the community in need of nonperishable food items. As of 2008, First Baptist and Templo Bautista Iglesia remained connected, with First Baptist providing physical and monetary support to the mission. First Baptist volunteers assisted with Vacation Bible School in July 2008, working with the mission congregation to share the message of Jesus Christ's love with neighborhood children.[185]

First Baptist reached out to the spiritual needs of Abilenians in other ways besides mission churches. During the first few decades of the twentieth century, First Baptist members sought to minister to businessmen staying in Abilene through a downtown Bible class on Sunday mornings. The idea of downtown Bible classes in America dated back to 1838, when the First Methodist Church of Chicago established the Arthur Dixon Bible Class. By the 1910s, the concept became very popular, and the Business Men's Class of Kansas City billed itself as the largest Bible class in the world.[186]

The men of First Baptist Church in Abilene liked the idea of a class dedicated to serving men, and established their own program on the second

Sunday of May 1919. The founders believed that Abilene needed a Bible class to minister to traveling businessmen who stayed in the downtown hotels on weekends. The class members chose to meet in a downtown theater (originally the Palace Theater), since such venues possessed the facilities to accommodate large crowds. The men of First Baptist also believed that a class in a theater might seem more open and attract people of all denominations and affiliations who would otherwise be deterred from attending a Sunday school class held at First Baptist or any other church. Through its efforts, the Victory Men's Bible Class ministered to the spiritual needs of men in the downtown area and sought "to reach men who do not go to Sunday School regularly in any church."[187]

Clyde Beasley attending the Victory Men's Bible Class

The class name served as recognition of the U.S. victory in World War I and the pride that the men felt as Americans. Judge J.P. Stinson, the first teacher of the class, recalled: "The war was barely over and we felt victorious, so we decided to call it the Victory Class."[188]

W.J. Behrens of Simmons College designed the order of service after one that he saw in California. The order of service for the class involved a specific set of events every week. These events included group singing, special music, prayers, presentation of the United States and Texas flags, and a class recital of the Pledge of Allegiance. The final parts of each week's services involved the introduction of all visitors to the class, followed by the day's Bible lesson. From the very first meeting, the same class members followed the same order of service, thus establishing continuity and making members as well as first-time visitors and intermittent attendees more at ease.[189] Also, hoping to reach as many as possible, the Victory Men's Class broadcast the service every week over a local radio station.

The class technically operated as a nondenominational entity. Even so, the Victory Men's Class maintained close ties with First Baptist Church and Simmons College. Starting with Jefferson Davis Sandefer, Simmons College presidents served as a part of the teaching faculty of the class for more than fifty years. Furthermore, all of the teachers were members of First Baptist.[190]

The membership of the class grew dramatically during its first four decades. Every Sunday, several hundred men met at the Palace and later the Queen theater, just a few blocks from the major hotels and First Baptist. The class proved so popular that prominent guest speakers regularly addressed the crowd. Speakers included U.S. Sen. Tom Connally, Texas Gov. Pat Neff, and Sam H. Cole, who was known as the King of the Hoboes. In 1922, U.S. Rep. William Upshaw reminded the class that while they were all businessmen and that business was important, religion and service to God remained more vital factors in life.[191]

Music was one of the most popular aspects of the class. In a large group setting, such as a formal worship service in a church sanctuary, some men felt nervous about singing. In a setting of other men, however, members of the class felt more comfortable about singing praises to God. To assist those attending the meetings with the songs and to encourage participation, the class published a small hymnal, "Songs of the Victory Men's Bible Class of First Baptist." The class motto, "Smile-Hustle," was prominently displayed on the cover.[192]

For several years, the Victory Men's Bible Class Orchestra led the music during the services. D.O. Wiley, a professor at Simmons College, led the orchestra. The music established such a reputation of excellence among the traveling businessmen passing through Abilene that WBAP, a prominent radio station in Fort Worth, asked the orchestra to perform a special show for broadcast over the radio.[193]

Although the class ministered to men, occasionally they allowed women to attend the services as well. One specific service that drew large crowds and included female participants took place on Mother's Day. Class members invited their wives to join the class as a celebration of their roles in the family. Father's Day services also proved popular, even though women were not invited that day. In 1935, five hundred fifty men attended the Father's Day service. On the special days that attracted such large crowds, the class moved to the nearby Paramount Theater to accommodate more people.[194]

The Victory Men's Bible Class also sponsored two social events each year: the annual banquet and the watermelon feast. Both were open to families and guests. Wives attended the banquet with their husbands, while families attended the watermelon feast. Class members also invited friends to the feast, thus allowing the event to serve as a recruiting tool. Watermelons remained a major attraction, as the class members put the fruit "on ice for four days." The men of the Bible class used the singing, games, entertainment, and ice-cold watermelon as points of contact with others in the Abilene community. The event provided members with opportunities to invite guests to attend the class and learn of unmet needs.[195]

Class members visited sick people in the local hospitals and their homes. A benevolence program provided clothes for underprivileged boys. Every Sunday, men from the Bible class went to the downtown hotels and throughout the lobbies and cafes to invite the guests to attend the class services.[196]

According to the members, one of the strongest points of the class was the Christian fellowship among men of diverse backgrounds and denominations.[197] Tom McWhirter described how he joined on his first Sunday in Abilene: "Leaving my hotel room, I started out for a walk and started past a theater, when I was stopped and greeted with the warmest welcome, the cheeriest smile and the firmest handclasp ever extended a stranger in any town." Along with the handshake, McWhirter's greeter extended "an invitation to visit with the Victory Men's Bible Sunday School Class."[198]

Over the years, interest and enrollment in the class changed. The majority of business travelers opted for newer lodgings in other parts of Abilene over the downtown hotels. Many businesses left downtown to adjust to the city's changing demographics. As a result, in 1967 the Victory Men's class moved from the Majestic Theater to the First Baptist Activities Building. The class also changed its name to the Victory Men's and Women's Bible Class, as many elderly couples attended the class together. However, the class continued to broadcast its services on the radio. The radio ministry began on station KFYO in 1939 and continued for sixty-nine years until the class disbanded. Furthermore, by meeting in the activities building instead of the main church building,

Final Meeting of the Victory Men's Class, 2007. Seated: Dr. Lewis Lemmond (class teacher), Dr. B.C. Roberson, Bobbie Lemmond. Standing: Cecil Gann, Keith Lloyd, Bill Bradshaw, Herb Roberts, Harold Wicker, J.L. Edwards, Sherwin McNair, Kermit Newton, Gaye Newton, Jerry Cunningham, Mary Cunningham, Winston Gann, Jim Sturrock.

the class kept its focus on members who might feel uncomfortable attending a church Sunday school class.[199] With the construction of the First Baptist Family Life Center in 1980, the class moved its location again.

In February 2007, the mission efforts of the Victory Men's Bible Class ended. Dr. Lewis Lemmond, who taught the class since 1983, retired. Members sought unsuccessfully to find a replacement teacher. As a result, after 87 years of service, members of the Victory Class issued a notice stating that with "membership and attendance declining due to deaths and ill health, members present on March 25, 2007 agreed that the class had fulfilled its original purpose and voted to disband."[200]

Through the mission work of First Baptist, the spiritual needs of the Abilene community were met. The numerous mission churches and the Victory Men's Bible Class provided outlets for people to worship, regardless of their background. As a result, the church stayed true to its founding ideal that it would be the *first* Baptist church in Abilene, not the only one.

Chapter 4

"Love Lifted Me"

Beginning in 1968, First Baptist Church undertook a dramatic shift in its mission to meet the physical and spiritual needs of Abilenians. The change began with the report by Tom and Marilyn McMillan that outlined specific needs faced by city residents. Pastor James Flamming used the report to help define First Baptist's role in Abilene as a downtown church. Since the neighborhood around the church, as well as all of society, had changed in the ninety-year history of First Baptist, Flamming and others in First Baptist believed that the congregation needed to develop new programs to serve the local community. The change of focus led to the establishment of four mission outreach programs that played major roles in serving the community.

The first of these programs grew directly out of the report issued by the McMillans. Maewyn Herring, one of the forty people who helped the McMillans compile the needs of Abilene, later recalled that when the groups drove around town, the "main thing we saw were children that were in need."[201] Particularly glaring was the lack of day care facilities, especially for low-income families.

Providing a place for children during the day was not a new idea at First Baptist. Starting in 1968, the church held a Mother's Day Out program on Fridays. Mothers could bring their children to the church for preschool activities, giving parents free time to shop, take care of jobs that needed to be done, or just relax.[202]

Inaugural GLO Board: Back row from left: A.E. Fogel, Mrs. Sondra Rosengrants, Leland Kelley, Lester Vinson, Mrs. J.R. Black, Jr., Ed Vaughn. Front row from left: Mrs. Maewyn Herring, Mrs. Roy Manahan, Guy Shaw, Mrs. Lillie Campbell, Mrs. Fike Godfrey

The Mother's Day Out program, however, only provided care one day a week and therefore did relatively little for working mothers. Abilene had a dearth of safe places for impoverished families to send their children during the workweek. In such families, both parents worked in order to meet financial obligations, or a single mother worked to support her children. As a result of changing social and economic conditions in Abilene and nationwide, parents needed affordable, quality child care.

Allie Ward, a retired teacher from Carter G. Woodson Elementary, the formerly segregated school in Abilene, ran one of the only day care facilities in town at the time. In her home, Ward cared for eight children whose mothers worked as custodial staff at various places. When First Baptist decided to open a day care facility, twelve women from the church visited Ward's home to observe her approach and acquire her feedback. Using this knowledge, First Baptist Church opened its day care center in December 1969.[203]

From the beginning, the church wanted the program to be an officially licensed day care. To meet this goal, the leadership of the day care met with representatives from the state mental health association, Texas Child Resources, and the state health board to make sure that the program met all state codes and requirements. Church members Robert Alvis and Guy Shaw, both licensed and practicing lawyers, established what Herring called a nonprofit "umbrella" for the day care that allowed the program to comply with state directives and thus be "official."[204]

The directors of the day care sought a name that did not specifically say "First Baptist Church." The group decided on the name "God's Little Ones," with the program eventually becoming known as GLO. First Baptist held an orientation in February 1969 to enlist support among church members and to train volunteers.[205]

When GLO officially opened in December 1969, Herring served as chairwoman of the board of directors, and Monett Gossett as the first director. Gossett worked as director for the first spring term only, leaving when she and her family moved. HSU student Barbara Hossenback served as the interim director during the summer of 1970. In the fall, GLO hired Geneva Rogers as director. Rogers served in the position for almost thirty years.[206]

In the beginning, GLO employed only three paid workers: Rogers, her assistant, and a cook. First Baptist members volunteered their time to cover the rest of the work. Numerous women and teenagers gave their mornings and afternoons to teach, read stories, or simply help with the children. Stella Fogle played piano for the music period each day. Marie Ramsey and Dotty Meadows devised menus each week covering the breakfast, morning snack, lunch, and afternoon snack for each of the children. Mary Webb baked a cake each month for all of the kids with birthdays that month and then held a birthday party for the recipients, complete with balloons and decorations. Others stopped in after work to help with cleanup, which involved washing bed linens and clothing, straightening up, and disinfecting toys with bleach solution.[207]

When GLO began, the preschool immediately ministered to a need in the community, but soon the program's own needs became apparent. Teachers dealt with as many of these as possible, such as the intense heat common during West Texas summers. GLO held daily "swim" sessions on the church

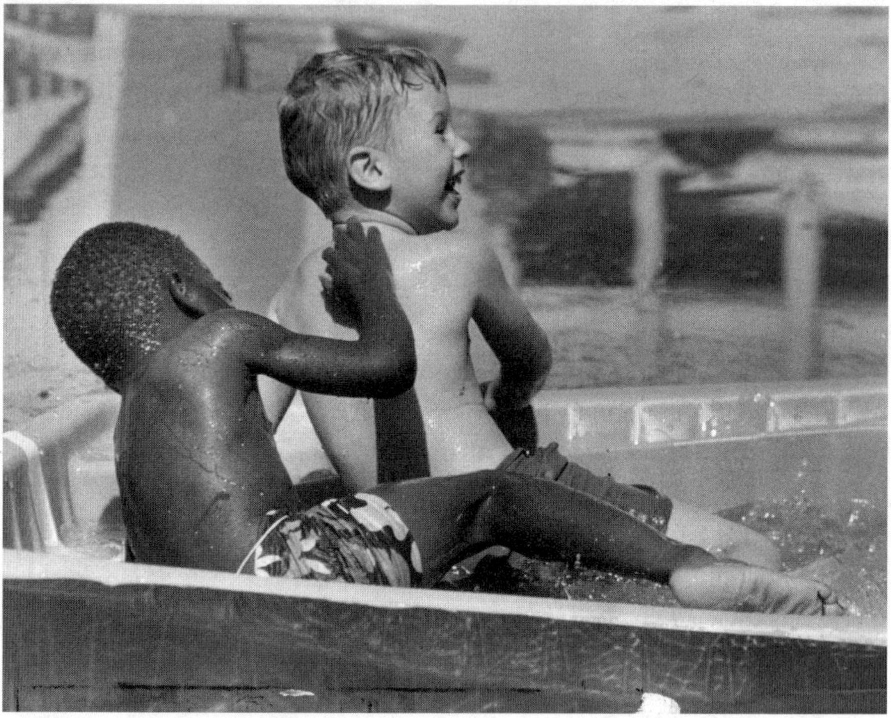

Two young men enjoy a GLO Swim Day

patio, with children splashing in wading pools and running around in sprinklers. For other needs, the program director appealed directly to the church membership. Early on, several specifics emerged, including little girls' dresses and shoes, training pants and little boys' play shorts, and volunteer teachers. Children's minister Carol Greenfield wrote in the church newsletter that "the need for training pants is never-ending."[208]

Larger issues also developed. Since GLO admitted both babies and older children, the program needed cribs to ensure a safe sleeping space for infants. The GLO board of directors appealed to Claude Hicks, director of Hendrick Home for Children. Hicks donated enough beds for all of the babies, and members of the First Baptist WMU sewed sheets for the beds. The church also donated all other furniture for GLO. Unfortunately, the children's furniture needed painting. Herring, Shirley Flamming, and Beth Walker stripped and painted all of the furniture. Herring remembered, "We probably had the most colorful nursery and kindergarten of anybody."[209]

Joy Davis assembling cribs donated to GLO by Hendrick Home for Children

When GLO opened in December 1969, seven children attended the first week. The number increased to nine by the next week, with fifteen attending through the summer. In the fall of 1970, thirty children from low-income families enrolled in GLO. The enrollment fee was pro-rated, based on the parents' weekly income and the number of their children registered. The program's success was evidenced by the fact that every class was at full capacity by November 1969, and the director kept a waiting list of names of children and families hoping to be accommodated. In addition to the regular day care classes, GLO enrolled ten older preschool children of Latino heritage in a program designed to teach English so the children would be better prepared to start school. At the same time, donations from First Baptist members continued to arrive, including a freezer, a refrigerator, games, toys, and clothes.[210]

The GLO program was unique in Abilene. It provided not only a place for kids to stay during the day but also an environment where the children received a Christian-based education. As part of the curriculum, Dolores Shaw and other volunteers taught pre-reading skills and numbers to prepare the students for first grade and later success in the public schools. Furthermore, GLO enrolled children of all ethnicities, a feature that made the program even more unique, considering that integration only came to Texas and the South following the Civil Rights Movement of the 1950s and 1960s.[211]

Although GLO's mission work focused on the children in the program, the families also benefited. Members of the board of directors visited every student's home. The educational services served as a way to discover other unmet needs, and First Baptist worked with GLO to meet those needs whenever feasible. Also, in its first five years of operation, GLO orchestrated a parenting program. The board required every parent to attend classes on nutrition, hygiene, basic medical and dental care, and how to help older children with homework.[212]

Geneva Rogers (standing) and GLO staff

News of GLO's success spread among Baptist churches in Texas and the rest of the nation. On May 12, 1970, Lloyd Henderson, the director of Texas Baptist Christian Social Missions, brought ten people to Abilene to observe GLO's program. The visitors wanted to research the possibility of establishing weekday missions in Baptist churches throughout Texas. Henderson and his group chose GLO as the model because the program was one of the few of its kind in the nation that ministered to economically disadvantaged families.[213]

The commitment of First Baptist members to the mission work of GLO was strong. With a volunteer staff, the teachers at GLO rotated to some extent. Many mothers with school-age children served as the first group of teachers. As the summer of 1970 arrived, though, the leaders of the program asked for new volunteers. Many of the regular teachers found themselves unable to work because they needed to be home with their own children during summer vacation. One group that GLO leaders targeted as volunteers was First Baptist's teenagers. GLO asked the young people not only to work with the children in the program but also to serve food, clean and organize closets, answer phones, and do basic office duties. The teenager involvement allowed the young people to use their natural abilities to assist GLO and involved the entire church body in the ministry.[214]

GLO teacher Jami Enfield and a student build with blocks

The national attention and praise for the work at GLO continued into the 1970 school year. In September, S.C. and Maewyn Herring represented First Baptist Church at the annual Christian Life Commission Workshop at the First Baptist Church of Houston. The workshop focused primarily on the work of GLO in the Abilene community. The Herrings served as speakers and gave a presentation on GLO's activities. The conference also allowed members of other Texas churches to ask questions about the program and request materials on starting similar programs in their cities. The success and appeal of GLO extended the influence of First Baptist's missionary spirit far beyond Abilene.[215]

Part of GLO's appeal lay in the potential as a point of contact with largely unchurched families. The annual Christmas dinner touched the lives of the children and their parents. Every year, First Baptist members hosted the event in the activities building. The children enrolled in the day care provided the evening's entertainment, performing a special program for their parents. Meanwhile, the GLO board of directors worked as hosts and hostesses, serving food and waiting on tables. The meal always included a full Christmas dinner, complete with turkey and dressing.[216]

In 1972, First Baptist organized a special Thanksgiving appreciation dinner for the GLO families and staff. As with the Christmas banquet, the directors provided the food and served the guests. For entertainment, the

Young girls pretend to be acrobats as part of GLO circus day in the recreation building

children enrolled in the GLO program dressed as Native Americans and Pilgrims and dramatized "The First Thanksgiving."[217]

By November 1972, thirty-six children participated in GLO, with an average daily attendance of thirty-three students. The program also received support from organizations in the community. The same month as the Thanksgiving banquet, the children at GLO were the guests of a "three-ring circus" that visited Abilene.[218]

The idea of a day care center for working families appealed to numerous Abilenians because of GLO's success. In the spring of 1973, Maewyn Herring and Rogers served as the guest speakers at the May Fellowship Day Luncheon of Church Women United. Sponsored by Aldersgate Methodist Church, the luncheon took place at First Christian Church and brought together women from throughout the community. The message given by Herring and Rogers concerned the mission work at GLO and the long waiting list of people wishing for their children to attend. Herring and Rogers concluded by discussing ways to get other churches to start day care centers for low-income working mothers.[219]

In response to this appeal, the Junior League of Abilene voted to create a similar day care. In April 1973, the league approved twenty thousand dollars for a two-year project. In conjunction with GLO, the Junior League established a day care center at the Ambler Street Baptist Mission to serve up to thirty children ranging in age from infancy to five years.[220]

The Ambler branch of GLO operated until August 1975. Control of the center shifted to Ambler Baptist Church when the church became independent. As a result, the program continued, but not as part the GLO budget.[221]

The majority of GLO activities focused on preparing children for school and on religious instruction. Other activities sparked the children's interest in nature and connected them with their community. The students went on field trips, had picnics at city parks, visited the Abilene Zoo, and had "paint days" during which they dressed in smocks and created large works of art. In the September 1973 monthly report, Rogers relayed a story of someone catching a horned toad that became a class pet. In order to care for the lizard, the children hunted red ants to "secure food for the horned toad, but he died anyway."[222]

Over the years, many features of GLO changed. The program originally was housed in the First Baptist recreation building in the former YMCA structure. By the late 1970s, however, the program relocated to the main church building. GLO gradually became part of the church budget instead of receiving its funding only through private donations. By 2008, GLO employed a director, a full complement of teachers, and a full kitchen staff. Enrollment continued to increase annually, with one hundred thirty students in 2008. Almost thirty years after its founding, GLO still served as an important outreach to the Abilene community. The reason, Maewyn Herring stated, was that although numerous for-profit day cares existed in Abilene by the start of the twenty-first century, "they keep the child, they feed the child, but they don't teach the child like we teach the child. Ours is a Christian-based educational unit."[223]

In 1977, as GLO continued to develop and thrive, a second outreach program emerged from the McMillan report and Flamming's call to action. First Baptist looked to help the emotional needs of the community with the creation of a counseling program. Directed by Everett V. and Marcine Reneer, the Ministry of Counseling and Enrichment originally sought to address the growing problem of divorce in America. Therefore, the Reneers initially focused on marriage counseling and met clients in the classrooms in the church's Educational Building.[224] However, the need for more types of counseling quickly became apparent. Since the ministry was a church-based, community-oriented program, it quickly provided a full range of counseling services to individuals, couples, and families.[225]

Like GLO, the Ministry of Counseling and Enrichment served as a model for other churches. By 1987, with 37,000 churches associated with the Southern Baptist Convention, the First Baptist Abilene Ministry of Counseling and Enrichment stood as the largest of its kind, but with a difference.

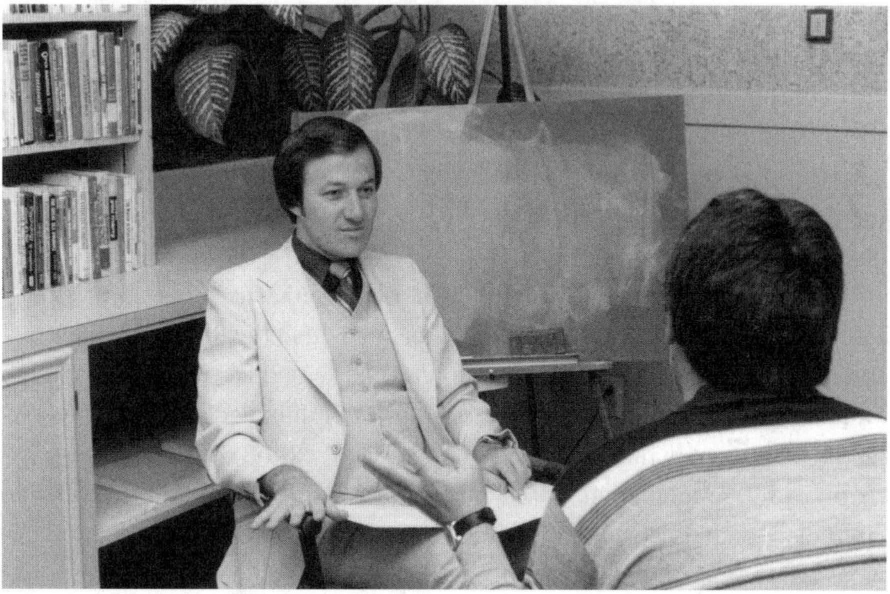

Mike Stedham at work at the Ministry of Counseling

Several large churches in Texas, including First Baptist of Houston and First Baptist of Dallas, possessed counseling ministries, but their centers served only the members of the church. The Abilene program provided services to people throughout the area, regardless of religious beliefs or church affiliation. During the program's first ten years, twenty-eight hundred families received counseling, of which less than twenty percent attended First Baptist.[226]

Mike Stedham joined the Ministry of Counseling and Enrichment in 1978 and took a leadership role in reaching out to meet the emotional needs of the Abilene community. During the early years, the ministry's offices in the church Education Building doubled as Sunday school rooms. On Mondays, Stedham removed the class tables and chairs and met clients throughout the week, and then on Saturdays rearranged the rooms to accommodate Sunday morning activities.[227] Despite the lack of space, the program grew. In 1979, Flamming concluded that the ministry had "succeeded beyond expectations."[228]

Also in 1979, the Ministry of Counseling and Enrichment moved across the street into a small brick building purchased by the church. The ministry remained in the building for fifteen years. Operating out of its own building allowed the ministry to expand and extend its reach, providing an inviting place

Ministry of Counseling and Enrichment (photo by Tiffany Fink)

for those who might have been uncomfortable seeking emotional or relational guidance in the main church facilities.[229]

By 1996, the building needed significant renovations. In response, First Baptist members voted to build a structure on a lot given to the church by the Guitar family. Located on North First Street near the main church building, the lot once hosted the Guitar family mansion, a historic building in Abilene, but the site had been unoccupied since 1964. The new Ministry of Counseling and Enrichment building included private offices for adult counseling, a children's area, large rooms for training and group meetings, and an administrative area.[230]

As Abilene's needs changed, so did the ministry's programs. The ministry added career planning workshops and divorce adjustment groups. Grief support groups, men's and women's groups, a suicide survivors support group, and a job transition group all reached out to specific areas of need.[231]

By 2008, fifteen full- and part-time therapists carried out the work of the Ministry of Counseling and Enrichment. Changes and additions continued to enhance the program. A children's counseling ministry grew out of the family ministry. At the facility on North First Street, the ministry established the

The children's therapeutic playground at the Ministry of Counseling and Enrichment (photo by Rob Fink)

"Children's Place." The building included two therapeutic play rooms with adjacent observation rooms. Also, First Baptist built a covered therapeutic playground to further enhance the mission efforts of the program as the well-being of children and families remained an important focal point for the ministry.[232]

Following up on the concerns for families in the Abilene area addressed by the Ministry of Counseling and Enrichment, First Baptist looked into another new ministry in 1979: a Family Life Center. The recreation ministry and recreation building dated back to the 1950s. By the late 1970s, however, the old recreation building required significant attention. As a result, First Baptist looked into constructing a modern facility where families could exercise, fellowship, and strengthen relationships, all in a Christ-centered environment.

With the idea for a Family Life Center approved, the church organized a committee to raise money and inform members about the goals and mission

First Baptist Church Family Life Center (photo by Tiffany Fink)

opportunities of the proposed center. In 1980, the committee published a magazine that outlined the center's goal: to allow all families in the Abilene community the opportunity to come together in a relaxed atmosphere and get more "family time" in a creative fashion. The fact that the facility would be open to all area families and would not exist simply as a private club for First Baptist members proved to be the deciding factor of support among many members. First Baptist, ever mission-minded, desired a Family Life Center where all were welcome.[233]

The committee focused the outreach efforts on two groups: the unchurched population and those who had needs that were going unmet within the church and Abilene as a whole. According to the committee, the Family Life Center would provide a "place where the physical, emotional, social, and spiritual qualities of life can be improved."[234]

As the plans progressed, some changes took place. The building committee issued a report that explained how it scratched an earlier idea for a formal reception room. Committee members found that most people expressed

David Leyerle oversees construction of the Family Life Center

Andrew and Dylan Fink use the bowling lanes at the Family Life Center, 2008 (photo by Tiffany Fink)

apprehension about braving the West Texas weather in the spring and summer to cross the street from the church sanctuary or chapel in order to attend a wedding reception. Furthermore, potential brides were dismayed at the thought of a wedding reception occurring next door to recreational activities such as bowling. The building committee suggested that the church use its dining room for receptions instead.[235]

However, the committee did endorse the idea of bowling facilities in the Family Life Center. Apparently some church members questioned the need for such facilities because several public bowling alleys opened in Abilene in the late 1970s. The committee responded by stating that the new lanes made First Baptist's bowling facilities even more necessary: since the Family Life Center focused on providing positive family fellowship, its bowling lanes were the only tobacco- and alcohol-free public facility in town.[236]

Flamming supported the Family Life Center in a "Pastoral Report" in August 1979: "The new Family Life Center is a tool for reaching people, for assisting families, for personal development, and for enhancing fellowship of our people . . . A downtown church has got to stay in the tug and pull of where people are, where their interests lie, and reach them as they are."[237]

With the plans and mission goals outlined, First Baptist broke ground on the new building on September 5, 1979.[238] Two years later, on March 8, 1981,

Young people playing in the Family Life Center game room during the Round-Up Sunday festivities, 2008 (photo by Tiffany Fink)

the church dedicated its new center during the morning worship hour. Afternoon and evening open houses allowed people to examine the building and equipment.[239]

Over the years, the Family Life Center provided numerous activities for family togetherness and community interaction. Youth and adult basketball leagues connected people from all socioeconomic and racial backgrounds. The center's First Place cafe provided good yet inexpensive lunches and suppers. Bowling tournaments, skating parties, and weekly handball games allowed First Baptist to reach out to the Abilene community. Through the youth sports, the idea of strengthening families grew as parents coached, ate with, and cheered for their children.[240]

Many of the community outreach efforts at the Family Life Center stemmed from David Leyerle. Hired as recreation minister in 1978, Leyerle, who previously served at a similar post at Walnut Street Baptist Church in Louisville, Kentucky, served First Baptist for almost thirty years. Leyerle focused the Recreation Ministry in three areas: to undergird the existing or-

Paper football tournament held in the Family Life Center skating rink

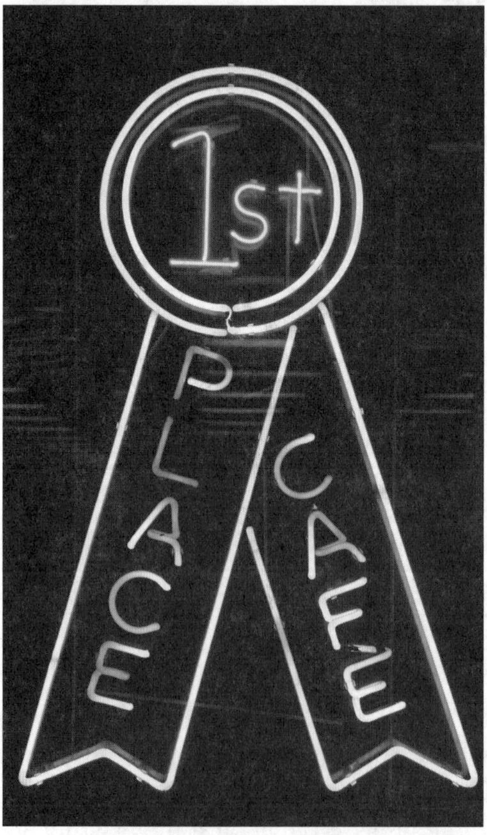

The First Place neon sign (photo by Tiffany Fink)

ganization of the church; to involve as many people in the church, not just through participation in recreation activities but in leadership positions; and to reach out to the community.[241]

The Family Life Center became highly successful. According to Leyerle, the ministry's success came from the fact that, as director, he was not locked into serving one specific age group or interest group, or even just the church membership. The result was a wide range of activities and opportunities that attracted a variety of people. Leyerle remembered, "I tried to use sports as the central way to draw people in because it would give me the largest numbers of people . . . Then, once they were in, they could find out about day camps, parties, and other activities."[242]

Ultimately, the FLC offered numerous events that served as points of contact with local residents. Leyerle recalled that, at one time, more than fifty basketball teams existed at the church, ranging from youth leagues to adult teams. The deacons sponsored a fish fry on Saturday nights during September, October, and November. The Family Life Center program hosted morning Bible studies, a Valentine's Day banquet, ski trips, and excursions to places such as Williamsburg, Virginia. Other events included racquetball tournaments, craft classes, birthday parties, and road trips for professional sporting events involving Major League Baseball's Texas Rangers or the National Football League's Dallas Cowboys. The key, Leyerle stated, was the diversity of the opportunities and how the programming provided reasons to come to the center.[243]

Two notable aspects of the Family Life Center were the First Place Restaurant and the Friday Family Fun Nights. The First Place provided a small grill area where people congregated, purchased food such as hamburgers and french fries, watched television or the basketball court, and fellowshipped. In the First Place, the diversity of the center's patrons was obvious as people of all economic and ethnic backgrounds ate and conversed. On the Friday Family Fun Nights, people gained access to all of the center's facilities for five dollars per family. Attendance averaged anywhere from one hundred to as many as two hundred fifty people.[244]

All of these points of contact assisted First Baptist in its larger goal of sharing the gospel. While non-members came with their children for basketball games or birthday parties, they also learned about Bible studies at the FLC and heard about Christ's resurrection. As a result, Leyerle stated, during the 1980s and early 1990s the Family Life Center was the first point of contact with approximately two out of every five people who joined the church without any prior connection to First Baptist.[245]

As time passed, new FLC programs emerged to serve the community outside the scope of recreation. Leyerle sought to take people beyond just basketball and skating. One significant program was the Big A Club. Originally an idea promoted by the national Women's Mission Union, the Big A Club focused on children in the first through fifth grades who might not attend a church and/or might need a positive influence. Knowledge of the Big A club spread mainly through word of mouth, beginning with the children and families who frequented the Family Life Center.

Every Wednesday night, the Big A leaders went out in church vans, picked up the children, and brought them to the Family Life Center. The children participated in a Bible study and a recreation activity and received a meal. The children in the Big A Club received a T-shirt and learned the club motto

Big A Club cookout at Celebration Park (photo courtesy of Leah Jeffries)

and the club handshake, which involved making a capital "A" with their fingers. The club also sponsored various events, including trips to Texas Rangers games and canoe trips on the Clear Fork of the Brazos River. After several years, the program expanded to include the Middle School Saturday Night Special program for sixth-, seventh-, and eighth-grade students, along with a high school program. Most important, many of the Big A children came to accept Jesus Christ as their Savior through the program.[246]

Another service of the Family Life Center involved its connection to the church's benevolence ministry. The FLC's locker room facilities provided a place for people to bathe who possessed no other access to running water. Furthermore, by providing employment opportunities ranging from full-time office or kitchen work to one-time tasks like taking out the trash, Leyerle and the church provided jobs to people who otherwise might not have had them.[247]

As the Family Life Center grew and greater opportunities arose to cultivate connections with Abilene's less fortunate, it became apparent that the FLC was not fulfilling its original purpose. FBC leadership discussed the issues and determined that the situation necessitated the creation of a new entity. First Baptist Church, then, hired Rob Rankin as Director of Recreation Ministry. Through Rankin's leadership and later, Scott Cook, the FLC became increasingly refocused toward recreation ministry. Scott Cook described his vision for the FLC, asserting that recreation ministry provided the community with "a common ground-an opportunity to build relationships."[248]

With the FLC focusing specifically on recreation ministry, a new outreach program was started to take over the benevolence programs. The birth of City Light Community Ministries, widely known as simply City Light, marked the fourth major mission outreach program started by First Baptist during the late twentieth century. Leyerle, who possessed a deep passion for urban ministry, left the FLC to direct City Light. City Light officially opened in 1996.[249]

Because it grew out of existing benevolence programs and activities at First Baptist, City Light originally operated out of the Family Life Center. The new ministry continued the FLC's far-reaching approach to service. City Light's programs and activities addressed a wide array of issues and were not tied to a specific program or group. "The church had a ministry that was open to people who were hurting," Leyerle said. He further added that the goal of the ministry was to seek the city's welfare, to "reach out to the least of these," and to identify and fulfill community needs that were not being met.[250]

City Light served as the coordinating agent of the church's benevolence programs. Most of the programs were already in existence, but they moved under a community missions heading, with a director and program to supervise implementation. At the Family Life Center, homeless people continued to receive access to showers. Beginning in 1997, the ministry administered a sack lunch program during the week for people who needed food. In addition, the Big A Club as well as the middle school and high school groups at the FLC moved under the direction of City Light.[251]

In 2001, City Light moved into a separate building, making the coordination of the mission activities easier and more efficient. To house City Light, First Baptist used a small, vacant bank one block north of the church. The church originally purchased the structure as space for Sunday school classes, but decided to convert the building into a mission center. During the next several years, members volunteered their time and money for the renovation of the building, which First Baptist had acquired in the late 1990s. Improve-

City Light Community Ministry building (photo by Tiffany Fink)

ments and renovations included staff offices, bathroom and shower areas for men and women, a laundry service area, a computer center, and a sizable dining area with a kitchen equipped to serve large numbers of people.[252]

The donations of time, energy and talents from First Baptist members became an essential element in the renovation. More than one hundred people participated in the project. Leyerle recalled Roy Jones and a group of men wielding sledgehammers and knocking out walls in the basement to create a large activity area. Mai-Lu Castle represented another example of church members' commitment to City Light. Castle served for many years as the cook in the First Place. When she passed away in the late 1990s, Castle bequeathed her life insurance policy of sixty-four thousand dollars to City Light Community Ministries. In memory of Castle's dedication to feeding and serving others, First Baptist used the gift to build and equip the kitchen at the new location.[253]

Much like other mission programs pioneered by First Baptist, City Light was unique within the community. Other local organizations and programs provided food, clothing, or assistance to those in need, but nothing in Abilene included the religious education focus of City Light. The benevolence pro-

City Light Sack Lunch Program (photo courtesy of Leah Jeffries)

grams at City Light, like the FLC's sports programs, served as points of contact for providing religious education in what Leyerle called a "tangible, intentional, structured way."[254]

Leyerle made several services available to City Light's clients. As church members prepared for the renovation of the First Baptist sanctuary in 2004, Leyerle employed several men in need of work to break down the old pews. The men then built crosses, end tables, coffee tables, and picture frames out of the wood, and Leyerle made these items available for sale. The efforts yielded significant results. The men received wages for their hard work and craftsmanship; the profits, which totaled seventeen thousand dollars, went toward the sanctuary renovation costs. Leyerle recalled that the project fostered a sense of accomplishment and satisfaction in those men who came to City Light for assistance and received much more. The money from the project strengthened the connection between the mission focus of First Baptist and the outreach programs at City Light. The action, as Leyerle recalled, epitomized the Christian outreach of City Light.[255]

The mission outreach to Abilene continued to grow as City Light expanded the existing sack lunch program, added staff, and further extended programs into the community, especially downtown. In 2002, Leyerle recruited Scott and Leah Jeffries to join the City Light team. The Jeffries felt the call of Jesus Christ to minister in home missions. City Light provided opportunities for the couple to work in the ministry's various programs and to create and administer new ones.

The adaptation of programs to meet the city's changing needs was one of the most effective aspects of the ministry of City Light. Although the sack lunch program helped provide for Abilenians, Leah Jeffries, who was the City Light Kitchen Coordinator from 2002 to 2006, felt that the program needed tweaking. She observed that most of the patrons left upon receiving their lunch instead of staying and visiting at City Light. Jeffries therefore prepared a large pot of beans to accompany the sack lunches, in the hope that patrons would stay to eat in the City Light dining room instead of taking the lunch "to go." The alteration worked, giving City Light volunteers a greater opportunity to form connections with participants, learn about further needs, and develop deeper relationships that often resulted in sharing the gospel of Jesus Christ on a daily basis. The program epitomized First Baptist's efforts to minister to both the physical and spiritual needs of Abilene residents as well as those who were just passing through the city.[256]

The success brought on by adding beans to the sack lunch program resulted in other changes in the City Light programs. The lunch program went from a schedule of five days a week to three days a week. Under the new setup organized by Leah Jeffries, clientele received a sack lunch one day, a hot meal prepared by Jeffries and the City Light team another day, and a hot lunch prepared by a First Baptist Sunday school class on Fridays. Patrons stayed to eat in the dining room, allowing for interaction with volunteers. The hot meals became the point of contact with many in the community that allowed City Light volunteers to reach out and meet a wide range of physical and spiritual needs. As Jeffries recalled, "People came to City Light, not to get a handout, but because they felt cared for."[257]

The lunches allowed members of First Baptist to have contact with people whom they might never have met otherwise. For the Sunday school classes, the experience was also a source of enjoyment. The Adult 1 Men's class participated monthly and sought to provide a better meal than any other class helping. Scott Jeffries recalled that the most important aspect of the

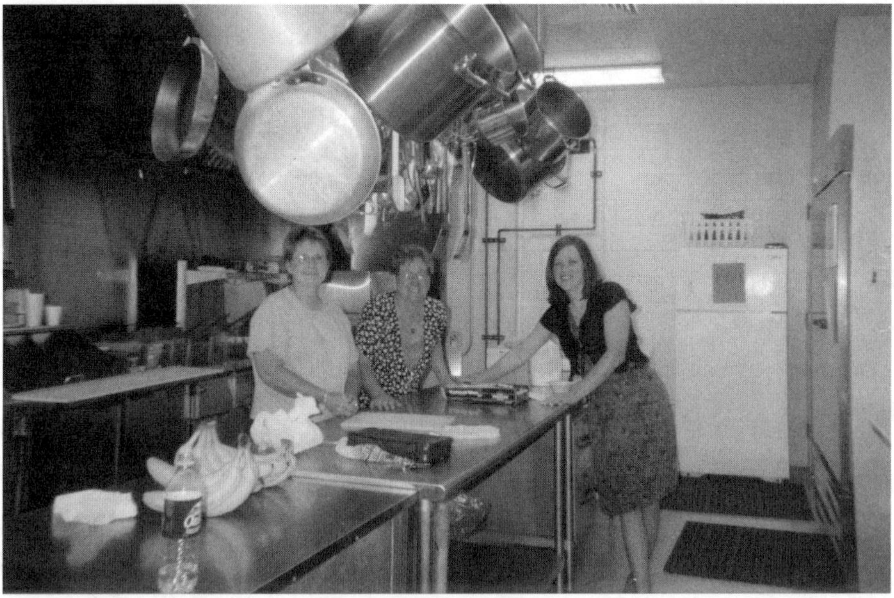

Teresa Crawford, Lynn Martin, and Leah Jeffries in the City Light Kitchen (photo courtesy of Leah Jeffries)

lunches came from the fact that the interaction "broke down barriers" between different groups in the community.[258]

The lunch program's success produced yet another ministry opportunity. Once per month, City Light hosted Agape dinners. Volunteers picked up attending families in church vans. The family-style meal involved the passing of food around the table in bowls. A short Bible lesson accompanied the meal. After dinner, the children went to the Family Life Center or the City Light basement for a recreation time, while the adults participated in games and fellowship, such as sing-alongs and dominoes.[259]

The previously existing mission programs at First Baptist that were coordinated by City Light, including the Big A Club and middle school and high school programs, also prospered. Through the ministry of the lunch program and the Big A Club, new needs in the Abilene community became apparent, and more programs began at City Light to meet them. An apartment ministry at the government-operated Vogel and Pioneer apartments served people who might not possess the means to travel to City Light. Volunteers used church buses to pick up children and families and take them to different activities at City Light. On Sunday mornings, City Light hosted its own church

The first Thanksgiving breakfast at City Light, 2002 (photo courtesy of Leah Jeffries)

service during the First Baptist Sunday school time, averaging between forty and fifty attendees.[260]

Beginning in 2003, City Light offered breakfast to anyone in the community on Thanksgiving Day. Volunteers worked alongside the ministry team and served approximately seventy people each year. Members of First Baptist and others in Abilene participated in the annual holiday breakfast in a variety of ways, often donating food and sitting down to break bread with those with no family nearby or no means to travel.[261]

The connections resulting from these activities allowed City Light Community Ministries to meet a wide range of physical and spiritual needs in Abilene. Through the assistance of City Light volunteers, a homeless, disabled, elderly man underwent cataract surgery, something he would not have received without the help. The ministry team connected a mentally handicapped woman with a social welfare caseworker, leading to her admittance to a nursing home. These cases were indicative of the assistance given through City Light on a daily basis. People received aid with bus fare, rent money, and utilities bills. "People need things but don't know how to get it," Leah Jeffries said.[262]

Scott and Leah Jeffries (second and third from left) participate in the City Light Sunday morning worship service (photo courtesy of Leah Jeffries)

Vernon Davis, former dean of the Logsdon School of Theology at Hardin-Simmons University, visited the City Light hot meal program one afternoon. Upon his return to the campus, Davis immediately contacted Scott Jeffries, who worked as a librarian at the university. Davis was awestruck by the ministry taking place at City Light and remarked to Scott: "That Leah, she's the pastor of those people!"[263]

Although most of the outreach of City Light focused on the homeless, the ministry also aided others. Through the City Light computer lab, church volunteers such as Scott Jeffries and Beverly Lenoir taught classes on basic computer skills. The clientele for these classes ranged from the elderly who knew nothing about computers but wanted to e-mail relatives to manual laborers who wanted to learn computer skills to acquire new jobs.[264]

Another effort not directly associated with the homeless population was the Rockin' Moms program. Peter Norton, an obstetrician and gynecologist in Abilene, came up with the idea for an outreach ministry targeting single mothers. Norton, Leyerle, Leah Jeffries, and Teresa Crawford (who was a City Light volunteer as well as one of the single mothers within the ministry), met in 2003 and planned the program.

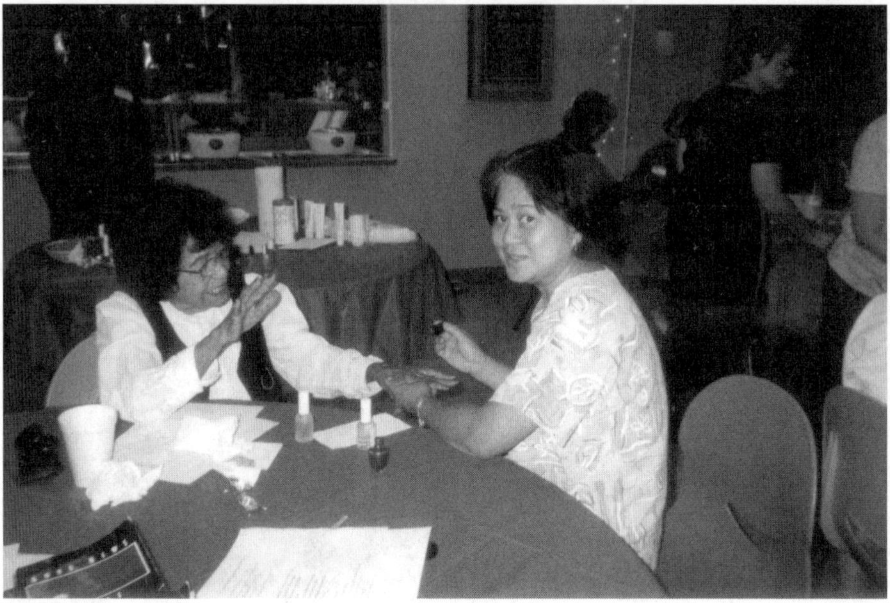

Rockin' Moms manicure night (photo courtesy of Leah Jeffries)

Rockin' Moms focused on the unique needs of single mothers. Some of the women were patrons of the lunches or other services provided by City Light, but many came only for Rocking Moms' meetings. The meetings occurred on the second Tuesday of each month, and City Light and First Baptist volunteers provided fellowship and a few hours' respite for mothers who did not have anyone else in their lives to assist in the care of their children. Twenty mothers attended the first meeting; through word of mouth, the regular attendance grew to an average of fifty to sixty women, ranging from teenagers with children to women raising their great-grandchildren. Although Rockin' Moms appealed largely to single mothers, volunteers welcomed any woman who wished to attend.[265]

At the meetings, the mothers and their children received a meal, and then the children went to the church nursery or participated in a recreation activity while the mothers took part in fellowship activities. Many of the activities focused on life skills like cooking, tax preparation, child care, and budgeting. One of the more popular events involved manicures for the moms.

Different groups of women from First Baptist volunteered to help in various capacities. Leah Jeffries and Maura de la Cruz often gave devotionals.

Marsha Jeffries teaches a cooking class at a Rockin' Moms meeting (photo courtesy of Leah Jeffries)

Beverly Cunningham frequently provided piano accompaniment for the sing-along portion of the evening. Diane Cole presented a program about how to dress for success in applying for jobs and how to determine which colors were most flattering for each individual woman. Katrina Fink told participants about strategies to help children succeed in the classroom. Marsha Jeffries demonstrated how to make healthy, budget-friendly meals using only a slow-cooking pot; the program ended with the presentation of a new pot to each woman in attendance.[266]

The appeal of Rockin' Moms was the warmth and camaraderie that permeated the room at each meeting. Through the years, the women, who were largely strangers to one another in the beginning, formed personal connections and a network of support. Women relayed concerns, exchanged ideas, and provided comfort and support for one another.

In the spring of 2008, City Light began an International Ministry in conjunction with a new Missions Committee at First Baptist. The International Ministry worked to assist hundreds of refugees from around the world who arrived in Abilene each year. Another new ministry effort included a senior adult Bible study. As a result, City Light boasted more than seventeen mission programs by 2008.[267]

The ministerial outgrowth of the 1968 report by Tom and Marilyn McMillan and the stirring charge later issued by Pastor James Flamming reached far beyond Abilene's city limits. GLO inspired several similar programs in Texas. The Ministry of Counseling and Enrichment provided guidance to people who carried their experiences outside of Abilene on a yearly basis. The Family Life Center continued to expand with new sports programs, exercise opportunities, and annual events and even provided job opportunities for students at Hardin-Simmons University, linking a relatively new church ministry to a much older effort. City Light Community Ministries, the fourth ministry developed from the call to action in 1968, continued to grow and expand, spreading light into neglected corners of the city, using love to lift those in need.

Conclusion

From its inception, First Baptist worked to serve the people of Abilene. Groups such as the Women's Mission Union, the Girls' Auxiliary, and the Willing Workers continually answered the call to service when needs arose. This service, like baking desserts for the soldiers' center during World War II, might have seemed inconsequential, but such acts played a major role in shaping the spirit and culture of Abilene.

The church's mission work produced important institutions that provided vital community resources. Through the vision of First Baptist members, Abilene acquired its first university, a move that established the town as an educational leader in the region. West Texas Baptist Sanitarium/Hendrick Memorial Hospital brought excellent medical care to West Texas. Through the continued support of First Baptist, through programs like the Hendrick Auxiliary and the Mother's Day fund as well as support from church members employed at the hospital, the church met the health care needs of thousands. Through its support of the Hendrick Home for Children, First Baptist provided a safe haven for the youngest members of society.

First Baptist's dedication to spreading the gospel of Jesus Christ shaped the spiritual climate in Abilene. As the town's population increased and developers established new neighborhoods, First Baptist sponsored mission churches to serve the residents. Although these actions might have reduced the overall membership of First Baptist, the congregation believed that it was more important to take the gospel to the people than to bring people to First Baptist. Members of the Victory Men's Bible Class epitomized the concept of becoming tangible extensions of Christ's love in the city where they lived, worked, and raised their families.

Finally, through the mission-minded outreach programs of the 1970s, 1980s, and 1990s, First Baptist refocused its efforts to continually serve the

Abilene area. GLO provided a nurturing, Christian atmosphere in which children could develop. The Ministry of Counseling and Enrichment and the Family Life Center sought to strengthen families in the community while also adapting and adding programs to meet the changing needs of the populace. Finally, City Light Community Ministries accepted the charge to serve those not represented by existing ministries, both at First Baptist and within the city. As a result, individuals and families, no matter what their shape, size or makeup, found themselves with a new place to belong.

In 2008, First Baptist again sought to refocus its role in Abilene. Building on the ideas expressed by James Flamming in 1969, the church focused on its mission outreach and position as a downtown church. But for one of the oldest churches in town, this was a recommitment instead of a new frontier. Long-time FBC member, Maewyn Herring even remarked, "We have always been missional."[268]

A key component of the recommitment involved envisioning the church's role in the twenty-first century. This self-examination meant exploring the definitions of mission outreach, reviewing the institution's history, and providing tangible examples to the church membership of how to apply these principles in each person's daily walk with Christ. The central issue revolved around developing an understanding of being missional versus being mission-minded. Dr. Phil Christopher, Senior Pastor of First Baptist Church since March 1995, summarized the approach, saying "It's not either/or. It's both." He went on to explain that, "[Being missional] becomes a lifestyle. Wherever we are we bring the Kingdom."[269]

First Baptist's 2008 recommitment to mission work provided a refocusing of the church's efforts. The physical and spiritual nature of Abilene has always changed and will continue to do so. The recognition by First Baptist of its mission heritage and its continued call to serve the community allows the church to build on the long history of service by its members. This legacy is the bedrock upon which future mission work will grow.

Appendix A

Pastors of First Baptist Church of Abilene, 1882-2008

1882-1883	L.S. Knight
1883	W.A. Whittle
1883-1886	Bennett Hatcher
1886-1889	G.W. Smith
1890-1892	J.C. Wingo
1892-1899	R.T. Hanks
1899-1901	Isaac Sellers
1901	Owen C. Pope
1901-1908	Lee Scarborough
1909-1912	C.C. Coleman
1913-1915	R.A. Kimbrough
1915-1948	Millard A. Jenkens
1948-1949	Jesse J. Northcutt
1950-1953	James L. Sullivan
1953-1966	Elwin L. Skiles
1966-1983	James Flamming
1985-1994	Bill Glenn Bruster
1995-present	Philip L. Christopher

Appendix B

General Chronology of Events in the History of First Baptist Abilene[270]

1881	Owen C. Pope and T.R. Legett organized Abilene First Baptist Church
1883	First sanctuary dedication
1885	Ladies Aid and Mission Society organized
1891	Abilene Baptist College established in cooperation with Sweetwater Baptist Association; later became Hardin-Simmons University
1892	Oak Street Mission started; later became South Side Baptist Church
1905	Blanche Rose Walker served in China as the first foreign missionary sent from First Baptist Abilene
1906	Valley View Mission established; later became Calvary Baptist Church
1910	Second sanctuary dedication
1915	Millard Jenkens accepted call as pastor, serving thirty-eight years
1920	E. Grady Hargrove became educational director
1924	West Texas Baptist Sanitarium opened; later became Hendrick Medical Center
1928	First Baptist Abilene hosted its first Vacation Bible School
1929	First Sunday School building dedication
1931	Sunset Mission organized; later became Elmwood Baptist Church
1938	Friendship Mission organized; later became Friendship Baptist Church; Brick Plant Mission organized
1939	Hendrick Home for Children founded
1944	Radio ministry inaugurated for broadcasting of worship services
1949	Cherry Street Mission organized; later joined with Friendship Baptist Church

1951	Sears Addition Mission organized; later became Ambler Street Baptist Church
1953	Elmwood West Mission organized; later became Pioneer Drive Baptist Church
1954	Third Sanctuary dedication at location of present sanctuary; Crescent Heights Mission organized; later became Crescent Heights Baptist Church
1958	Lakeside Mission organized near Lake Fort Phantom
1969	God's Little Ones Day Care Center opened
1974	Television ministry inaugurated for broadcasting worship services
1977	Ministry of Counseling established
1981	Dedication of the Family Life Center
1987	Lytle South Baptist Mission organized; later became Lytle South Baptist Church; Ash Street Mission organized in conjunction with Holiday Hills Baptist Church
1988	Quail Valley Mission organized
1989	Abilene Associational Social Ministries Mission organized in cooperative effort with the Abilene Baptist Association; First Baptist Church Foundation established
1990	Hispanic Mission organized; later became Templo Bautista Iglesia
1993	Solid Rock Baptist Mission organized
1995	PrayerWorks Ministry inaugurated
1996	Ordination of the first women as deacons of First Baptist Abilene
1997	City Light Community Ministries established
2004	Therapeutic Playground opened at the Ministry of Counseling
2006	Fourth sanctuary dedication following renovations; dedication of the Shelton Organ

Notes

[1]Katharyn Duff, *Abilene . . . On Catclaw Creek: A Profile of a West Texas Town* (Abilene: The Reporter Publishing Company, 1969), 3, 11.
[2]Tommie Clack with Katharyn Duff, "Recollections of Miss Tommie Clack," in *Pioneer Days . . . Two Views* (Abilene: Zachary Associates, Inc., 1979), 135.
[3]Duff, *Abilene*, 48.
[4]Ibid., 49.
[5]Ibid., 51.
[6]Ibid., 51.
[7]Ibid., 56.
[8]Ibid., 57, 59, 61, 63.
[9]Mary Hampton Clack, *Early Days in West Texas*, reprint in *Pioneer Days . . . Two Views* (Abilene: Zachary Associates, Inc., 1979), 96.
[10]Clack, "Recollections," 205; Duff, *Abilene*, 79.
[11]J. Edward Gray, "The History of the First Baptist Church of Abilene, Texas," Thesis: Hardin-Simmons University, MA, August 1957, 1.
[12]Owen C. Pope, "Texas Baptist Herald," 19 January 1882, published in *The First Baptist Advance*, 26 January 1951.
[13]Duff, *Abilene*, 79.
[14]Gray, "History of First Baptist Church," 3-4.
[15]Ibid., 4-5.
[16]Ibid., 5, 9, 10.
[17]Ibid., 7-8.
[18]Byers Petty, "Notes from the History of W.M.U.-First Baptist," 1976, First Baptist Church archives.
[19]Duff, *Abilene*, 79.
[20]*Holy Bible*, (New International Version).
[21]Gray, "History of First Baptist Church," 13.
[22]"Missions and Abilene First Baptist Church," First Baptist Church archives.
[23]"Sunday School Class Reunion Held at Birthday," *Abilene Reporter News*, 13 March 1949; *Report of the Willing Workers*, 1 January 1898, First Baptist Church archives.
[24]Gray, "History of First Baptist Church," 15.
[25]Ibid., 16.
[26]Duff, *Abilene*, 89, 120.
[27]Ibid., 174.
[28]"Highlights of the Past-Baptist Women," First Baptist Church archives.
[29]Gray, "History of First Baptist Church," 18-19.
[30]"Highlights of the Past-Baptist Women," First Baptist Church archives; Mrs. Byers Petty, "Notes from the History of W.M.U.-First Baptist," 1976, First Baptist Church archives.
[31]Gray, "History of First Baptist Church," 21; Rupert N. Richardson, "The Abilene Baptist Story," First Baptist Church archives.
[32]Gray, "History of First Baptist Church," 27.
[33]Ibid., 44.
[34]Petty, "Notes from the History of W.M.U.-First Baptist."
[35]Duff, *Abilene*,205.
[36]Juanita Daniel Zachary, *Abilene: The Key City* (Northridge, California: Windsor Publications, Inc., 1986), 63.
[37]Gray, "History of First Baptist Church," 21.
[38]Ibid.
[39]Ibid., 77.

[40]Zachary, *Abilene: The Key City,* 81.
[41]Ibid., 81-82.
[42]Gray, "History of First Baptist Church," 87, 92.
[43]Ibid., 27.
[44]Ibid., 113-114.
[45]Duff, *Abilene,* 221.
[46]Untitled History of First Baptist, First Baptist Church archives.
[47]Tracy Shilcutt, David Coffey, and Donald S. Frazier, *Historic Abilene: An Illustrated History* (San Antonio: Historic Publishing Network, 2000), 53; Gray, "History of First Baptist Church," 130; Maewyn Herring, interview by Rob Fink, 19 June 2008, Abilene, Texas.
[48]Gray, "History of First Baptist Church," 130; "Soldier Center to be Opened and Dedicated," *The First Baptist Advance,* 29 May 1943.
[49]"Baptist Soldier Center Weekly Schedule," First Baptist Church archives; Gray, "History of First Baptist Church," 130.
[50]"On Mother's Day be a Mother to Some Soldier," *The First Baptist Advance,* 7 May 1943.
[51]"First Baptist Church Special Prayer Service," 19 April 1944, First Baptist Church archives.
[52]"Highlights of the Past-Baptist Women," First Baptist Church archives.
[53]Ibid.
[54]Ibid.
[55]Paul Lack, Robert Sledge, Fane Downs, and Paul Jungmeyer, *The History of Abilene: Facts and Sources* (Abilene: McMurry College, 1981), 2.
[56]Shilcutt, *Historic Abilene,* 59.
[57]"Resolution Authorizing Trustees to Execute Contract for Purchase of YMCA Property," 29 August 1956, First Baptist Church archives.
[58]N. Alex Bickley, President, Smith, Bickley, and Pope, Attorneys at Law, letter to E.A. Shepperd, 24 July 1956. First Baptist Church archives.
[59]"Basketball Tournament Begins," *The First Baptist Advance,* 11 January 1957
[60]*The First Baptist Advance,* 25 October 1957.
[61]Minutes, First Baptist Church, December 1960, First Baptist Church archives; Minutes, First Baptist Church, November 1961, First Baptist Church archives.
[62]Untitled History of First Baptist, First Baptist Church archives.
[63]"Church to have KRBC-TV Devotionals," *The First Baptist Advance,* 4 January 1957.
[64]Letter from Idus V. Owensby to Reverend and Mrs. James Alexander, March 8 1957, First Baptist Church archives.
[65]"Ministry for Deaf-Mutes to Begin at First Baptist," *Abilene Reporter News,* November 1959. First Baptist Church archives.
[66]"Highlights of the Past-Baptist Women," First Baptist Church archives; Untitled History of First Baptist W.M.U., First Baptist Church archives.
[67]Letter from Dr. Stanton J. Barron, 1968, First Baptist Church archives.
[68]D. Warren Craik, letter to Mrs. Jeannie A. Branch and Randy Branch, 24 March 1960, First Baptist Church archives.
[69]"Application for Charter," National Office, Boy Scouts of America, 1963, First Baptist Church archives.
[70]"1st Baptists, St. Paul Eye Race Polices," *Abilene Reporter News,* 13 September 1963.
[71]*The First Baptist Advance,* 27 October 1966.
[72]"Clothes Bank Report for 1964," *The First Baptist Advance,* 19 February 1965.
[73]Don Lewis, "Baptist Clothing 'Bank' Gives Garments to Needy," *Abilene Reporter News,* 18 August 1957.
[74]Petty, "Notes from the history of W.M.U.-First Baptist," 1976, First Baptist Church archives.
[75]"Memorial Service: A Community Moving Toward Unity in Christ," 7 April 1968, First Baptist Church archives.
[76]Herring, interview by Rob Fink, 19 June 2008, Abilene, Texas.

[77]Ibid.
[78]"From the East Window," *The First Baptist Advance*, 26 September 1969.
[79]Ibid.
[80]Ibid.
[81]Ibid.
[82]*The First Baptist Advance*, 7 May 1970; *The First Baptist Advance*, 28 May 1971.
[83]Memo from Television Study Committee to the Members of First Baptist Church, 17 March 1974, First Baptist Church archives.
[84]"Television Committee Recommendations," 15 September 1974, First Baptist Church archives.
[85]"Pastoral Report," August 1979, First Baptist Church archives.
[86]Ibid.
[87]"FBC Benevolent Ministry Policies," May 1982, First Baptist Church archives.
[88]"Report to the Benevolence Committee," March 1980, First Baptist Church archives.
[89]"Committee Report Sheet First Baptist Church," Benevolence Committee, 1 July 1981, First Baptist Church archives.
[90]*First Baptist Edition of the Baptist Standard*, 11 March 1981.
[91]*First Baptist Edition of the Baptist Standard*, 7 October 1981.

Notes From Chapter 2:
[92]Gray, "History of First Baptist Church," 27.
[93]Duff, *Abilene*, 152.
[94]Gray, "History of First Baptist Church," 27.
[95]Duff, *Abilene*, 153.
[96]Clack, "Recollections," 214.
[97]"Missionary Society Minutes," 19 October 1890, First Baptist Church archives.
[98]Clack, "Recollections," 215.
[99]Ibid.
[100]Ibid.
[101]Ibid., 217.
[102]Ibid., 215.
[103]Thurman Morrison, *Music at Simmons: The First Fifty Years, 1892-1942* (Abilene: Hardin-Simmons University Press, 1974), 1.
[104]Gray, "History of First Baptist Church," 29.
[105]Duff, *Abilene*, 155.
[106]"Missions and Abilene First Baptist Church," First Baptist Church archives.
[107]"First Baptist Church Abilene," 27 April 1988, WMU Centennial File, First Baptist Church archives.
[108]Vernon Gladden Spence, *Judge Legett of Abilene: A Texas Frontier Profile* (College Station: Texas A&M University Press, 1977), 119.
[109]Gray, "History of First Baptist Church," 46.
[110]Ibid., 34
[111]Morrison, *Music at Simmons*, 44, 48.
[112]Gray, "History of First Baptist Church," 65.
[113]A. Yvonne Stackhouse. *Hardin-Simmons University: A Centennial History* (Abilene: Hardin-Simmons University, 1991), 123.
[114]Gray, "History of First Baptist Church," 71, 74.
[115]Ibid., 30.
[116]Morrison, *Music at Simmons*, 73-74.
[117]Duff, *Abilene*, 121.
[118]Morrison, *Music at Simmons*, 82, 123.
[119]Rupert Richardson, *Famous are Thy Halls: Hardin-Simmons University as I have Known It* (Abilene Printing and Stationery: Abilene, 1976), 137, 141, 143.

[120]*The First Baptist Advance*, 12 June 1943.
[121]"First Baptist Church Majors in Youth," *The First Baptist Advance*, 5 May 1946.
[122]Stackhouse, *Hardin-Simmons*, 123.
[123]Ibid., 222.
[124]"Dr. Flamming's Acceptance of Call is Good News," *The First Baptist Advance*, 27 October 1966.
[125]"Students in Homes," *The First Baptist Advance*, 26 October 1956.
[126]Stackhouse, *Hardin-Simmons*, 192.
[127]"Our First Fifty-Just the Beginning," speech, 1971, First Baptist Church archives.
[128]A.C. Greene, *A Personal Country* (College Station: Texas A&M University Press, 1969), 104-105.
[129]Gray, "History of First Baptist Church," 95.
[130]"Our First Fifty-Just the Beginning," speech, 1971, First Baptist Church archives.
[131]"Hendrick History," www.ehendrick.org/history.htm.
[132]"Hendrick History," www.ehendrick.org/history.htm; Gray, "History of First Baptist Church," 96-97.
[133]"Mother's Day Hospital Offering," *The First Baptist Advance*, 30 April 1954; *The First Baptist Advance*, 10 May 1957.
[134]"Honoring Mother," *The First Baptist Advance*, 10 May 1946.
[135]Betty Kay Seibit, *Millionaire Cowboy* (Abilene: Hendrick Home for Children, 1983), 40.
[136]Ibid., 40.
[137]"The Legend of the Black-eyed Pea," www.ehendrick.org/bpea.htm.
[138]Seibit, *Millionaire Cowboy*, 40.
[139]Oscar Kimsey Bowden, *Mr. Hendrick: Rancher, Oilman, Philanthropist* (Abilene: Hendrick Home For Children, 1962), 87.
[140]Bowden, *Mr. Hendrick*, 69, 87.
[141]Seibit, *Millionaire Cowboy*, 41.
[142]Ibid.
[143]Ibid., 42.
[144]Ibid.
[145]Our First Fifty-Just the Beginning," speech, 1971, First Baptist Church archives.
[146]Herring, interview by Rob Fink, 19 June 2008.
[147]Seibit, *Millionaire Cowboy*, 45.
[148]Bowden, *Mr. Hendrick*, 93, 94, 95.
[149]Ibid., 97.
[150]Seibit, *Millionaire Cowboy*, 52.
[151]Bowden, *Mr. Hendrick*, 98.
[152]"Whatever Happened to Gloria, Carl, Ray? Trusler Kids at Hendrick Home," in "Hendrick Home for Children: 40 Years of Love," Special Supplement, *Abilene Reporter News*, 22-23 June 1979, First Baptist Church archives.
[153]Katharyn Duff, "Hendrick Home," in "Hendrick Home for Children: 40 Years of Love," Special Supplement, *Abilene Reporter News*, 22-23 June 1979, First Baptist Church archives.
[154]Ibid.
[155]www.hendrickhome.com/Services.html

Notes From Chapter 3:

[156]"Some Historical Skitchings . . . ," First Baptist Church archives; Gray, "History of First Baptist Church," 34.
[157]"Missions and Abilene First Baptist Church," First Baptist Church archives.
[158]"Local Missions Established by First Baptist Church Abilene," First Baptist Church archives.
[159]"Local Missions Established by First Baptist Church Abilene," First Baptist Church archives; Gray, "History of First Baptist Church," 57.
[160]"Missions and Abilene First Baptist Church," First Baptist Church archives.
[161]Gray, "History of First Baptist Church," 58, 62.

[162]Ibid., 82-83.

[163]"Local Missions Established by First Baptist Church Abilene," First Baptist Church archives.

[164]Gray, "History of First Baptist Church," 141, 142; "Local Missions Established by First Baptist Church Abilene," First Baptist Church archives.

[165]"Missions and Abilene First Baptist Church," First Baptist Church archives; "Local Missions Established by First Baptist Church Abilene," First Baptist Church archives.

[166] "Missions and Abilene First Baptist Church," First Baptist Church archives; "Local Missions Established by First Baptist Church Abilene," First Baptist Church archives.

[167]Bowden, *Mr. Hendrick*, 92.

[168]"First Baptist Church Minutes on Friendship Mission," February 1938, May 1938, First Baptist Church archives; "Local Missions Established by First Baptist Church Abilene," First Baptist Church archives.

[169]Gray, "History of First Baptist Church," 122.

[170]Ibid., 142.

[171]"Satellite Agreement," Friendship Baptist Church, 1976, First Baptist Church archives.

[172]Gray, "History of First Baptist Church," 142.

[173]"Coming to Elmwood West . . . ," flier, First Baptist Church archives.

[174]Ibid.

[175]"Initial Service as Elmwood West Sunday," *The First Baptist Advance*, 30 April 1954.

[176]"Pastor's Paragraphs," *The First Baptist Advance*, 30 April 1954.

[177]Gray, "History of First Baptist Church," 143.

[178]*First Baptist Church Edition of the Baptist Standard*, 27 November 1974.

[179]"30,000 Award Received," *The First Baptist Advance*, 17 July 1959; "Mission Needs Rug," *The First Baptist Advance*, 9 December 1960.

[180]"Latin American Baptist Work in Abilene," *The First Baptist Advance*, 8 March 1963.

[181]"Ambler Baptist Pre-School," First Baptist Church archives.

[182]Tom McMillan, "To Tell the Secret," Report, Church Study, 1968, First Baptist Church archives; Roy Jones, "Ambler Baptist Mission to Gain Autonomy Sunday," *Abilene Reporter News*, 23 November 1974; *First Baptist Church Edition of the Baptist Standard*, 6 November 1974.

[183]"Local Missions Established by First Baptist Church Abilene," First Baptist Church archives.

[184]Informational material, "Lytle South" folder, First Baptist Church archives.

[185]"First Baptist Abilene, A Tapestry of Faith: The 125th Anniversary," Booklet, First Baptist Church Abilene, 2006.

[186]Jane Stinson Huff, "History of the Victory Men's Bible Class," Thesis: Hardin-Simmons University. MA, June 1948, 3, 15.

[187]Ibid., 26-28.

[188]Ibid., 27.

[189]Untitled History of the Victory Men's Bible Class, First Baptist Church archives.

[190]Huff, "Victory Men's Bible Class," 29.

[191]Ibid., 30-31.

[192]"Songs of the Victory Men's Bible Class of First Baptist Church, Abilene Texas" (Abilene: Abilene Printing Company, 1923), First Baptist Church archives.

[193]"Brief History of the Victory Men's Bible Class," First Baptist Church archives.

[194]Huff, "Victory Men's Bible Class," 34.

[195]Ibid., 35, 37

[196]Ibid., 38-39.

[197]Ibid., 45.

[198]Ibid., 67.

[199]"Victory Class Moves to Activities Building," *The First Baptist Advance*, 3 August 1967; "Brief History of the Victory Men's Bible Class," First Baptist Church archives.

[200]Notice, from Victory Class, First Baptist Church archives.

Notes From Chapter 4:

[201]Herring, interview by Rob Fink, 19 June 2008, Abilene, Texas.
[202]"From Carole," *The First Baptist Advance*, 5 September 1968.
[203]Herring, interview by Rob Fink, 19 June 2008, Abilene, Texas.
[204]Ibid.
[205]"GLO Orientation," *The First Baptist Advance*, 27 February 1969.
[206]Herring, interview by Rob Fink, 19 June 2008, Abilene, Texas.
[207]Ibid.
[208]"GLO is Now Operational," *The First Baptist Advance*, 15 August 1969; "From Carole," *The First Baptist Advance*, 15 August 1969.
[209]Herring, interview by Rob Fink, 19 June 2008, Abilene, Texas.
[210]*The First Baptist Advance*, 24 October 1969; *The First Baptist Advance*, 30 January 1970.
[211]Herring, interview by Rob Fink, 19 June 2008, Abilene, Texas.
[212]Ibid.
[213]"GLO Object of State Missions Department Study May 12," *The First Baptist Advance*, 7 May 1970.
[214]*The First Baptist Advance*, 21 May 1970.
[215]"GLO Day Care Center Featured at Christian Life Workshop," *The First Baptist Advance*, 24 September 1970.
[216]"Christmas Dinner for GLO Families December 13, 1971," *The First Baptist Advance*, 9 December 1971.
[217]"GLO Monthly Report," November 1972, First Baptist Church archives.
[218]"GLO Day Care Center Monthly Missions Report," November 1972, First Baptist Church archives.
[219]"Church Women to Meet Friday," First Baptist Church archives.
[220]"Junior League Votes $20,000 for Day Care Center Project," *Abilene Reporter News*, 12 April 1973.
[221]Lester Vinson, associate pastor, letter to Reverend Ruben Hernandez, 5 June 1975, First Baptist Church archives.
[222]GLO Board Minutes, 19 September 1973, First Baptist Church archives.
[223]Herring, interview by Rob Fink, 19 June 2008, Abilene, Texas.
[224]"Ministry of Counseling," First Baptist Church archives.
[225]"Ministry of Counseling and Enrichment: A Center for Personal and Family Growth," First Baptist Church archives.
[226]"Couple Provides First Aid for Shattered Lives," *Abilene Reporter News*, 19 September 1987.
[227]Ibid.
[228]"Pastoral Report," August 1979, First Baptist Church archives.
[229]"A Dream Realized: Ministry of Counseling and Enrichment," 1996, First Baptist Church archives.
[230]Ibid.
[231]"Couple Provides First Aid for Shattered Lives," *Abilene Reporter News*, 19 September 1987; Steve Queen, director, Ministry of Counseling, interview by Rob Fink, 12 June 2008, Abilene, Texas.
[232]Queen, interview by Rob Fink, 12 June 2008, Abilene, Texas.
[233]"A Family Life Center: For Family, Outreach, Fellowship, Development," First Baptist Church archives.
[234]Ibid.
[235]"Report from the Family Life Center Building Committee," First Baptist Church archives.
[236]Ibid.
[237]"Pastoral Report," August 1979, First Baptist Church archives.
[238]*First Baptist Church Edition of the Baptist Standard*, 5 September 1979.
[239]*First Baptist Church Edition of the Baptist Standard*, 4 March 1981.

[240]Scott Jeffries, e-mail to Rob Fink, 17 April 2008.
[241]David and Sharon Leyerle, interview by Rob Fink, 22 May 2008, Abilene, Texas.
[242]Ibid.
[243]Ibid.
[244]Ibid.
[245]Ibid.
[246]Ibid.
[247]Ibid.
[248]Scott Cook, interview by Rob and Tiffany Fink, 89 October 2008, Abilene, Texas.
[249]David and Sharon Leyerle, interview by Rob Fink, 22 May 2008, Abilene, Texas.
[250]Ibid.
[251]Ibid.
[252]Philip L. Christopher, E-mail to Rob and Tiffany Fink, 7 October 2008; David and Sharon Leyerle, interview by Rob Fink, 22 May 2008, Abilene, Texas.
[253]David and Sharon Leyerle, interview by Rob Fink, 22 May 2008, Abilene, Texas.
[254]Ibid.
[255]Ibid.
[256]Leah Jeffries, telephone interview by Rob Fink, 17 June 2008.
[257]Ibid.
[258]Scott Jeffries, telephone interview by Rob Fink, 16 June 2008.
[259]Ibid.
[260]Ibid.
[261]Ibid.
[262]Leah Jeffries, telephone interview by Rob Fink, 17 June 2008.
[263]Scott and Leah Jeffries, interview by Tiffany Fink, 29 June 2008, Grand Prairie, Texas.
[264]Scott Jeffries, telephone interview by Rob Fink, 16 June 2008.
[265]Leah Jeffries, telephone interview by Rob Fink, 17 June 2008.
[266]Ibid.
[267]*City Light News*, First Baptist Church, Abilene, Texas, 29 April 2008.

Notes From Conclusion:

[268]Herring, interview by Rob Fink, 19 June 2008, Abilene, Texas.
[269]Philip L. Christopher, Interview by Rob and Tiffany
Fink, 2 October 2008, Abilene, Texas.
[270]"First Baptist Abilene, A Tapestry of Faith: The 125th Anniversary," Booklet, First Baptist Church Abilene, 2006.

Bibliography

Books:

Bowden, Oscar Kimsey. *Mr. Hendrick: Rancher, Oilman, Philanthropist.* Abilene: Hendrick Home for Children, 1962.

Clack, Tommie/ Kathryn Duff. *Pioneer Days . . . Two Views.* Abilene: Zachary Associates, Inc., 1979.

Duff, Kathryn. *Abilene . . . On Catclaw Creek: A Profile of a West Texas Town.* Abilene: The Reporter Publishing Company, 1969.

Greene, A.C. *A Personal Country.* College Station: Texas A&M University Press, 1969.

Holy Bible, New International Version.

Lack, Paul, Robert Sledge, Fane Downs, and Paul Jungmeyer, *The History of Abilene: Facts and Sources.* Abilene: McMurry College, 1981.

Morrison, Thurman. *Music at Simmons: The First Fifty Years, 1892-1942.* Abilene: Hardin-Simmons University Press, 1974.

Richardson, Rupert. *Famous are Thy Halls: Hardin-Simmons University as I have Known It.* Abilene Printing and Stationery: Abilene, 1976.

Seibit, Betty Kay. *Millionaire Cowboy.* Abilene: Hendrick Home for Children, 1983.

Shilcutt, Tracy, David Coffey, and Donald S. Frazier. *Historic Abilene: An Illustrated History.* San Antonio: Historic Publishing Network, 2000.

Spence, Vernon Gladden. *Judge Legett of Abilene: A Texas Frontier Profile.* College Station: Texas A&M University Press, 1977.

Stackhouse, A. Yvonne. *Hardin-Simmons University: A Centennial History.* Abilene: Hardin-Simmons University, 1991.

Zachary, Juanita Daniel. *Abilene: The Key City.* Northridge, California: Windsor Publications, Inc., 1986.

Theses:

Gray, J. Edward. "The History of the First Baptist Church of Abilene, Texas," Thesis: Hardin-Simmons University, MA, August 1957.

Huff, Jane Stinson. "History of the Victory Men's Bible Class," Thesis: Hardin-Simmons University. MA, June 1948.

Booklets:

"First Baptist Abilene, A Tapestry of Faith: The 125th Anniversary," Booklet, First Baptist Church Abilene, 2006.

Newspapers:

Abilene Reporter News, 13 March 1949; 18 August 1957; November 1959; 13 September 1963; 12 April 1973; 23 November 1974; 22-23 June 1979; 19 September 1987.

City Light News, 29 April 2008.

First Baptist Advance, The. 7, 29 May; 12 June 1943; 5, 10 May 1946; 26 January 1951; 30 April 1954; 26 October 1956; 4, 11 January; 10 May; 25 October 1957; 17 July 1959; 9 December 1960; 8 March 1963; 27 October 1966; 5 September 1968; 27 February; 15 August; 24 October 1969; 30 January; 7, 21 May; 24 September 1970; 28 May; 9 December 1971.

First Baptist Edition of the Baptist Standard, 6, 27 November 1974; 5 September 1979; 4, 11 March 1981; 7 October 1981.

Interviews:

Christopher, Philip L.

Cook, Scott

Herring, Maewyn

Jeffries, Leah

Jeffries, Scott

Leyerle, David

Leyerle, Sharon

Queen, Steve

Material from First Baptist Church Archives

"A Dream Realized: Ministry of Counseling and Enrichment," 1996.

"A Family Life Center: For Family, Outreach, Fellowship, Development."

"Ambler Baptist Pre-School."

"Application for Charter," National Office, Boy Scouts of America, 1963.

"Baptist Soldier Center Weekly Schedule."

Barron, Dr. Stanton J. Letter, 1968.

Bickley, N. Alex, President, Smith, Bickley, and Pope, Attorneys at Law.

Letter to E.A. Shepperd, 24 July 1956.
"Brief History of the Victory Men's Bible Class."
"Church Women to Meet Friday."
"Coming to Elmwood West . . . ," flier.
"Committee Report Sheet First Baptist Church," Benevolence Committee, 1 July 1981.
Craik, D. Warren. Letter to Mrs. Jeannie A. Branch and Randy Branch, 24 March 1960.
"FBC Benevolent Ministry Policies," May 1982.
"First Baptist Church Abilene," 27 April 1988, WMU Centennial File.
"First Baptist Church Minutes on Friendship Mission," February 1938, May 1938.
"First Baptist Church Special Prayer Service," 19 April 1944.
GLO Board Minutes, 19 September 1973.
"GLO Day Care Center Monthly Missions Report," November 1972.
"GLO Monthly Report," November 1972.
"Highlights of the Past-Baptist Women."
Informational material, "Lytle South" folder.
"Local Missions Established by First Baptist Church Abilene."
McMillan, Tom. "To Tell the Secret," Report, Church Study, 1968.
Memo from Television Study Committee to the Members of First Baptist Church, 17 March 1974.
"Memorial Service: A Community Moving Toward Unity in Christ," 7 April 1968.
"Ministry of Counseling."
"Ministry of Counseling and Enrichment: A Center for Personal and Family Growth."
Minutes, First Baptist Church, December 1960.
Minutes, First Baptist Church, November 1961.
"Missionary Society Minutes," 19 October 1890.
"Missions and Abilene First Baptist Church."
Notice, from Victory Class.
"Our First Fifty-Just the Beginning," speech, 1971.
Owensby, Idus V. Letter to Reverend and Mrs. James Alexander, 8 March 1957.

"Pastoral Report," August 1979.
Petty, Mrs. Byers. "Notes from the History of W.M.U.-First Baptist." 1976.
"Report from the Family life Center Building Committee."
"Report of the Willing Workers," 1 January 1898.
"Report to the Benevolence Committee," March 1980.
"Resolution Authorizing Trustees to Execute Contract for Purchase of YMCA Property," 29 August 1956.
Richardson, Rupert N. "The Abilene Baptist Story."
"Satellite Agreement," Friendship Baptist Church, 1976.
"Some Historical Skitchings ...."
"Songs of the Victory Men's Bible Class of First Baptist Church, Abilene Texas." Abilene: Abilene Printing Company, 1923.
"Television Committee Recommendations," 15 September 1974.
Untitled History of First Baptist.
Untitled History of First Baptist W.M.U.
Untitled History of the Victory Men's Bible Class.
Vinson, Lester, associate pastor. Letter to Reverend Ruben Hernandez, 5 June 1975.

Web Sites:

www.ehendrick.org/bpea.htm.
www.ehendrick.org/history.htm
www.hendrickhome.com/Services.html

E-mails:

Scott Jeffries. E-mail to Rob Fink, 17 April 2008.
Philip L. Christopher. E-mail to Rob and Tiffany Fink, 7 October 2008.

Index